Language Remediation and Expansion

SCHOOL AND HOME PROGRAM

by Catharine S. Bush

Illustrated by
Don Bush

**Communication
Skill Builders, Inc.**
3130 N. Dodge Blvd./P.O. Box 42050
Tucson, Arizona 85733
(602) 327-6021

Copyright © 1980 by Communication Skill Builders, Inc.
3130 N. Dodge Blvd./P.O. Box 42050
Tucson, Arizona 85733

ISBN 0-88450-711-4
Catalog No. 3063

Foreword

Throughout twenty years of classroom teaching, parenting, developing and implementing individualized speech and language programs, giving workshops to parents, teachers and specialists, and learning from others, I have searched for the most effective and efficient means to remediate and expand language in students. My concerns have included motivating students, selecting and using materials and methods efficiently, involving parents in the language learning process, and developing useful cognitive, linguistic and communicative skills in each student.

This book presents a *framework* for developing communication skills in a pragmatic manner — using the students' natural interests, environment and life experiences as the stimuli and calling upon the families to help model, teach and reinforce. The program has been used successfully in several socioeconomic areas by specialists and teachers with varied backgrounds, techniques and experience.

We have found that using a *thematic* approach not only gives continuity and cohesiveness to learning, but it also offers an opportunity for contextual language practice at school and at home. The thematic approach also provides a method for introducing new concepts, information and vocabulary which can be related to previously learned material and thus more easily assimilated by the student. The program stresses experience-based language and communicative interaction for the elementary school-aged child. Each unit in the program contains ideas and exercises for developing skills in the areas of (1) phonology, (2) morphology and syntax, (3) semantics, (4) cognition, and (5) production of language.

This is not a step-by-step procedure for language learning or remediation. It is a *framework* within which the creative specialist or teacher may develop individual communication skills his or her students need. Modification techniques preferred by the professional may be used within the theme. Source and reference materials are included to demonstrate creative uses of each unit.

Suggestions are given for using stimulating visual and auditory environments, hands-on materials to provide tactile reinforcement, and simple parent-child activities for use at home. Also included are re-reproducible pages meant to save time for the teacher or specialist. Those pages so indicated may be reproduced for classroom or home projects.

The following pages explain the components of the program and how to prepare and proceed. Twelve units follow with the practical aspects of the School-Home Program and skill-building materials.

ACKNOWLEDGMENTS

Many thanks to Michele Bush for her creative ideas and to many of my colleagues who tried out the materials and offered useful suggestions.

Catharine S. Bush, CCC
Speech-Language Pathologist

Contents

PART I

School-Home Thematic Program

LIFE–EXPERIENCE THEMES

Twelve themes have been chosen and elaborated upon for use throughout the school year. You may wish to use each theme for two or three weeks, choosing those of current interest to you and the students, or those related to your curriculum. For instance, the unit on *Weather– Seasons–Time–Measurement* is useful in the winter because children are experiencing and are very conscious of seasonal changes, snow, and temperatures. That awareness is a good basis for the concepts in the unit.

The theme subjects begin with the child himself in the first unit and gradually spread out to his world, moving from concrete relationships (family, food, animals) to more abstract ones (space, communication, fantasy). In the presented order of the themes you will recognize a logical bridge from one unit to the next.

Using these life–experience units provides an alternative to the usual holiday themes which are presently used so extensively in the schools and are not always relevant or of interest to students of varied backgrounds.

Each theme is a starting point for introducing concepts and vocabulary in a relevant, contextual manner. These concepts serve as the raw material for skill-building experiences. Suggestions are provided for involving the parents and families in helping and stimulating the student. The families can and should contribute their ideas and experiences in conversations and activities. Thus learning is extended from the school setting to the home where reinforcement, practice and new information may be provided. The child's total environment becomes his learning ground.

USE OF THE PROGRAM

This thematic program has been developed and used in several different forms over the past ten years, with diverse student and family populations. The materials, activities and home experiences have been field-tested in multicultural areas, with various socioeconomic groups and with students on levels from kindergarten to the eighth grade.

Because life experiences are relevant to all students, the interest level has been high throughout the groups and consequently the gains made by the students have been excellent. Parents have proved to be eager, enthusiastic and effective in helping their children with the program activities.

The program allows for flexibility and creativity on the part of the specialist or teacher in meeting the individual language needs of students of differing ages and backgrounds. Those who field-tested the School-Home Program found it stimulated new ideas and new approaches to their work. They also observed that students were excited about the theme content and visual environment material. These and the hands-on displays encourage oral communication and cognitive functioning.

The materials and activities are designed for the remediation and expansion of language skills. Speech-language pathologists, learning disabilities specialists or cross-categorical specialists, and classroom teachers should find the program useful. It may be used with individuals, small groups or entire classes.

THEMATIC ENVIRONMENT

It is very important to set up a stimulating physical environment to make language learning meaningful, dynamic, contextual and useful. This includes using visual, auditory and tactile stimuli which have relevance to the topic at hand. The materials suggested in these units are versatile enough to appeal to students of various ages, thereby accommodating the specialist who serves several age groups.

Visual and Auditory

Each of the twelve themes provides a suggested visual background and related materials to attract the students' interest, to arouse curiosity and to provide topics for concept discussion and language practice. The murals and/or cutouts in the book may be enlarged to a convenient size with the use of an opaque projector or an overhead projector. Itinerant specialists or those in small working spaces may

wish to use murals or posters which may be attached to an easel or blackboard and removed easily for transport.

As you begin a theme, talk about the visual background and pose questions, varying the discussion according to the age and experience of the students. Encourage comments and questions. Labels, vocabulary words and questions may be attached to the background as you proceed with the theme. Colored index cards are inexpensive and very useful for making these and other word cards for displays and vocabulary games. The students may wish to bring pictures or objects from home to add to the background. For instance, in the *Transportation— Space* unit, you might hang student-made models near the mural.

Posters may also be used, such as those of animals in *Instructor* and *World* magazines or the thought-provoking posters on various subjects in *Learning* magazine. Some other excellent posters that are language-stimulating and fit in with the themes are to be found in the Peabody Language Development Kits. Pictures may also be cut out of the magazines recommended in the units and mounted on construction paper for use in skill activities. It is helpful to organize a filing system for storage of posters, mounted pictures, and ideas you conceive or find which can be utilized with each topic. Of course, the murals may be saved and used year after year.

Visual materials, such as food displays and window decorations, are sometimes obtainable from drug, grocery and department stores, which may donate the displays when they are no longer needed.

When introducing a new theme, phonograph records are effective in stimulating a mood (for example, electronic music for the *Transportation—Space* theme. Records also provide listening practice and stir the imagination. Once the child is immersed in the subject, he will find it easier and more exciting to participate in the language-learning activities and to think both divergently and convergently. Records are suggested for use with the units. Students should also be encouraged to bring in other records appropriate to the theme.

Tactile: Theme Displays

The theme displays are an important part of the language remediation and expansion program. Objects central to the theme — whether actual objects, miniature representations, or toys — should be displayed where they can be touched, discussed, labeled, categorized, rhymed with, compared, described, researched and even used for improvisations. Linguistic, cognitive and communicative tasks can center upon these hands-on materials. For instance, in the unit on *Weather— Seasons—Time—Measurement,* all kinds of timepieces and measuring instruments can be displayed. Time concepts are then discussed using the real objects and new vocabulary is introduced and reinforced by the tactile experience. The objects are described by the students for oral communication experience and specific language forms may be practiced with the objects as subject material. Dealing with real-life materials provides added interest and relevance to the tasks.

The items may be introduced a few at a time (especially in instances where the specialist is itinerant and must transport materials or lacks space in the room), or a display of all the objects may be set up at the introduction of the unit for use during the two- or three-week period. One specialist I know uses a colorful suitcase as her

traveling display case. The students eagerly look forward to seeing it and using its contents.

Students and families should be encouraged to bring items to be shared in the display. The child's name may be added as the contributor. This increases the school-home cooperative learning spirit and the students enjoy using their own familiar objects in skill-building exercises.

It is not difficult, time-consuming or expensive to collect the materials. Ask the PTA, room mothers, parent assistants in your program, or parents of students to help collect items you need. Objects may be purchased at garage sales or collected from toy boxes of family, friends and students. Familiar household objects, food packages, and items from the workshop or garage are useful. Ordinarily, the objects do not have to be in perfect working order. Other items can easily be made (for example, a flag, crown or fan made of paper). Each unit lists suggested items for one or more displays.

For convenient storage and retrieval of these language displays, ditto-paper boxes or other uniform-size boxes may be labeled with the unit name and stacked. (I found some sturdy ski-boot boxes at a sports store and the owner was glad to save them for me.) Because some objects may be used for more than one theme, keep an inventory of each box handy. You may wish to include relevant books, pictures and other materials in the theme box.

Other small objects may be used for language activities. A description of these is included in Appendix A.

VOCABULARY LISTS

The use of the theme vocabulary makes language study contextual, relevant and useful. Each unit has a vocabulary list drawn from the theme which can be used in many ways. The words are graphed for easy retrieval when teaching a certain skill, such as syllabication, multiple meanings, sound blending (phonemes), rhyming, compound words, or classification. Words may be selected for practice of beginning sounds, synonyms, or for articulation practice.

You may wish to put groups of words on charts for use in story writing, sentence construction, or vocabulary building games. Lists may be sent home for use in family activities, such as charades and word games, or for use in conversation to build vocabularies. Room is provided for additions to the lists. For instance, as you brainstorm words in categories (things you do with your feet, names of vegetables, etc.), add them to the theme vocabulary.

The skills lists in each unit contain suggestions for using the vocabulary and creating additional exercises for each skill. The words are on varied difficulty levels for extended use. Exposing the student to new words in context is valuable even if he is not ready to incorporate them into his expressive language.

The words that have a check mark in the *Rhyming* column on the vocabulary lists all have at least four possible rhyming words. Under the *Phoneme* column (used for sound blending), two-, three- and four-phoneme words are indicated.

BOOKS

Reading books and/or talking about them with children is essential in remediation and expanding language. This should take place both in the school program and at home. The students hear patterns of language, learn new concepts, relate new ideas to previous learning, and improve their comprehension, vocabulary and listening skills. Books can introduce a theme or be integrated with it.

Selected examples of well-illustrated books that have been found useful in the program have been suggested for each unit. All are readily available and generally inexpensive. You can recommend many of these to the parents for inclusion in the children's own libraries to be read over and over at home. A variety of other inexpensive books should be recommended to the parents in order that they may be given to children as presents, surprises or rewards, making books treasured possessions. We should encourage parents to read and talk about books often with the children in order to establish good reading habits.

Other books that relate to the theme can be checked out of the library for use during the unit. Students should be encouraged to bring theme-appropriate books and magazines which can be shared with their peers.

A list of books recommended for the professional using the program as well as a list for parent reading are included in Appendix C.

MATERIALS AND ACTIVITIES

Skill-building materials are suggested which fit in well with the theme in each unit. Some are commercial and the suppliers are indicated. Others may easily be made by your aides or by parents. Add to the materials lists names of other materials you have which relate to the units. As you find materials, pamphlets, plays, stories, pictures and other activity ideas, add them to your theme files for later use.

Activities which may be used during language sessions are also listed. Select ones that will be useful for reinforcing skills or teaching concepts needed in individual programs.

SKILLS LISTS

The School-Home Program is intended to be a framework within which the specialist or teacher can design and implement specific goals and exercises to meet the individual needs of students. Theme-related skills lists are included in the areas of *phonology, syntax and morphology, semantics, cognition* and *production of language* for each unit. You may draw from these as needed and add new items to the lists. The activities included in each unit will vary according to their usefulness within the theme. If you are concentrating on a particular skill (for example, rhyming, inferences or descriptive language), check through all the units to find additional practice items. Extended lists of exercises for each skill area can be found in *Language Remediation and Expansion: 100 Skill-Building Reference Lists.* * The list numbers from this companion volume are indicated for your convenience in each unit.

Language Remediation and Expansion: 100 Skill-Building Reference Lists by Catharine S. Bush (Tucson, Arizona: Communication Skill Builders, Inc., 1979).

Unit 1 is an expanded model unit which contains suggestions for teaching each language skill. For the sake of brevity, these instructions are not repeated in subsequent units. They are, however, applicable to them. There are additional activities and skill-building ideas suggested in the other units which could be utilized in any of the themes.

HOME PARTICIPATION

Parents and families play an integral part in developing and maintaining language skills in the child. We need to identify and clarify for parents their roles in the process and we must provide frequent communication on how they can help. They have many opportunities for intimate one-to-one communicative interaction, natural learning situations and experiences, providing skill reinforcement, expanding concepts, and shaping good attitudes toward learning. Most parents are eager to help but need and appreciate direction and concrete suggestions.

Parent Contacts

Individual conferences or group meetings should be held with the parents early in the program to explain their roles in the School-Home Thematic Language Program. Some parental responsibilities could include:

1. reading and talking about books with the child, visiting the library to find more information on the theme, sending theme-appropriate books or records with the child to school to be shared;

2. doing the suggested theme-related activities or exercises with the child (these would be listed in a letter to parents as each topic is introduced; see sample letters on pages 10, 25–26, 83, 114, 132, and 163–64);

3. using the suggested vocabulary words with the child in discussing aspects of the theme (these would be included with the home letter);

4. expanding upon each subject, having dinner table discussions (parents have a wealth of knowledge to share with their children and the themes help them focus in on a topic);

5. helping the child find and bring related objects for the display (when the child becomes the "expert" in sharing his object, his self-concept is enhanced and he finds communication practice rewarding);

6. taking the mini-field trips suggested for each unit and talking about what is seen and done, recalling later with the child the sequence of events and new things learned.

The specialist or teacher will want to determine home participation objectives tailored for the individual needs of her students.

If the parents miss the initial meeting, send a letter outlining the program and their participation and set up an alternate conference. Frequent contacts with the parents should be made through the home letters, parent visits to informal classroom events, and other parent

FAMILY WORD GAMES

participation activities (see page 11). Ask the parents to watch for the letters coming home with the student. You may wish to mail the home letters.

If you are writing Individual Education Plans (IEP) you can indicate that the School-Home Program will be used, and outline the parents' responsibilities on the IEP.

Letters to Parents

Send a letter home as you start each theme (samples are provided in several units). These letters have been used for students in kindergarten through fourth grades and the response has been excellent. Select and include activities most appropriate for your students' needs. You may wish to compose a separate letter with different home activities for older students. Specific directions for the child's individual needs or a progress report may be added to the duplicated letter.

If you are in a bilingual community, you may wish to translate the letter into a second language. We have had parents assist with this. Recognition of cultural differences will be appreciated by the parents, which helps in cementing relations with them.

To be sure that the parents recognize the letter, print it on colored paper if possible. Add a small illustration to add interest. Letters may also be hand-written on a ditto for a more informal approach. Attach simple materials for current projects, such as the interview sheet in the *Occupations* unit. The students usually look forward eagerly to taking the letter home because it means valued parent-child interaction will take place. Before sending the letter home, explain its contents to the students and encourage them to get started on their projects and to return them when they are finished.

Home Projects

Parents are encouraged to help their children with one or more brief projects for each theme. It may be an *interview* about occupations, a *survey* on a trip to the grocery store, brainstorming a *list* of sports, *making* a simple puppet, or *helping* the child with a skill-building exercise. These tasks should be simple yet enjoyable while emphasizing communicative interaction and expanding experience.

We have found that most parents not only help but report they enjoyed and expanded on the projects. When the child brings back his project and shares his experience, the school-home learning pattern is reinforced. The parents also see the value of their involvement as the child's skills increase. Soon the parents find that nearly every activity around the house or routine trip in the neighborhood can be the occasion for language skill development or vocabulary and concept-building as they interact with their child. The school-home thematic approach helps the parents maximize their efficiency in assisting their children.

Several ideas are listed in each unit from which you may choose those to be suggested in the home letter. Reproducible project pages are also included; these may be duplicated and sent home with the home letter.

SAMPLE LETTER

Dear Parents:

This year our language skill-building activities will be centered around a different theme every two or three weeks. I will send home a letter explaining each theme and will suggest related home activities to reinforce the school program. Please help your child by:

1. doing the <u>Home Projects</u> with your child and taking the suggested <u>Family Field Trips</u>. As each child shares his home project and home experiences with the class, he is developing self-confidence in his communicative ability and his self-concept.

2. using the suggested <u>vocabulary words</u> in your conversations. Children learn most of their words from natural discussions. Use new words with your child often. When you read to him or her, ask your child the meanings of new words to check comprehension.

3. expanding on the theme subject and creating new activities. Have <u>dinner table discussions</u> on our theme subject. Encourage each family member to talk and to listen attentively to others. Compliment them on their ideas.

4. helping your child find objects, books or records relating to our subject to bring to school for sharing and displays. For instance, if our subject is oceans and fish, you might send seashells you have found.

Your child will make much more progress when you are helping. Thank you for your cooperation. If you have any questions, please call me.

Sincerely,

Family Field Trips

In each unit there are some suggestions for family mini-field trips. These are generally to places within the neighborhood or area. As you use the theme for language study, the families can visit a park, grocery store, service station, pet store, construction site, or the parent's own place of work in order to learn new concepts and vocabulary and to increase oral language interchange. The parent has the opportunity to model language, to pose thoughtful questions, and to help develop the child's inquiring mind as they visit the sites together. Later they can recall things they saw and did, relate that information to other new ideas, and create stories about the trip.

The student can bring back to school information to contribute to the theme discussions. These concrete experiences are invaluable in building concepts. We need to help parents use daily activities as learning experiences for their children.

OTHER INVOLVEMENT OF PARENTS

To further encourage parent involvement in the student's language learning process, parents should be invited to participate in other ways. Their help can be valuable to the busy specialist or teacher. Possibilities include:

1. helping in the classroom or therapy room by reading to children, playing vocabulary games, or following through on planned tasks or programs;

2. helping to make materials for skills work;

3. collecting items for displays;

4. attending parent meetings or workshops to learn skills to help their children;

5. assisting at parent meetings;

6. attending short plays or programs put on by the students;

7. going on school-sponsored field trips with their children (this is not only a help to the specialist or teacher, but is most useful for home discussion afterward).

Many of these activities are not time-consuming and may be done by working parents at home. As the child observes his parent participating in the school program, he is likely to attach more importance to his school experience.

You may wish to have mini-workshops for parents on how to increase communication skills through family activities. We have found parents are very appreciative of this help and follow through well on the activities. Subjects for workshops might include (1) home activities for learning basic concepts, (2) books and reading with children, (3) language games at home for skill-building, (4) building listening and memory skills, and (5) expressive language activities. Try to arrange workshops or other class visits on an occasional evening in order to accommodate working parents.

A FISHY TALE

CREATIVE LANGUAGE

As students develop language skills, they should see the results transferred to the printed word. This helps build the child's self-concept as a communicator and provides another link in the school-home cooperative relationship when the child takes his stories home to be read. Intermingling reading, speaking, writing, body language, and cognitive tasks in the language program unifies and solidifies the learning of language skills.

Stories

Story shape cutouts which may be reproduced for story writing have been included in Units 1, 4, 5, 6, 7, 8, 9, 11 and 12. After the current theme has been explored and used, let the student dictate a theme-related story which you print on the construction paper cutout. You may help the child by asking, "What happened then?", "How did she look?" or "What did he say?" Students of all ages can participate in this activity. They can draw on or decorate the other side of the shape-story. Parents or older student assistants may prepare the cutout shapes for you.

Read the stories to the students, using lots of expression. Children enjoy hearing them. The students may even act out the stories. Send your young authors' stories home to be read, displayed and enjoyed by the families. Encourage the parents to save all the stories in a folder for the child to read at the end of the year. This will enable the parents to see the child's progress in the use of language.

Display the stories in the cafeteria, the office, or hallway as well as in the classroom for more positive reinforcement for the child. Set up a young authors' corner where students may enjoy one anothers' stories in spare moments.

The progress of one first grade student may be seen in these theme-related stories dictated to this author over a five-month period.

Animal theme — November
　　Once I had a horse. It was black. It fell down. He was big. He ate hay. He was nice. The end.

Transportation theme — February

One day I went up in a balloon. I was up high. A jet almost hit the balloon. Then the balloon was going down. It was spooky. It never came down. The end.

Monster theme — April

Once I was in a cave. I saw this green monster with purple eyes. I climbed on his tail and he felt me climbing. He looked back and he saw me. I smiled at him and he smiled back. He took me down to the beach and went in the water. We swam in the ocean for an hour. It was lots of fun. The end.

Notice the increased sentence length, the greater complexity of structure, and the improved story line from one story to the next.

The story shapes may also be used for creative writing stimulators. Print theme-related words on the cut-out shape and laminate it. Place it in your writing center. Students may compose stories using the words for spelling reference and ideas.

Language Charts

Make charts of words you brainstorm with the students for each unit. These are useful for other language activities. Print comments or questions that students have about the units on paper strips to be hung up in the room. Write experience stories with the students and display them. Transfer children's oral communication to printed words often.

ACTING OUT LANGUAGE

A sometimes overlooked but very important part of communication is nonverbal language. The thematic units emphasize the use of pantomime, gestures, and improvisation in the production of language. Using the body to interpret and convey concepts, vocabulary and sequences of ideas involves much cognitive planning and results in a firmer grasp of the material being studied. Antonyms, compound words, homonyms and rhyming pairs are good subjects for beginning pantomime. Many other subjects for nonverbal activities are listed in *Language Remediation and Expansion: 100 Skill-Building Reference Lists.*

Language is a social, interpersonal process; acting out language for and with others facilitates this process. Students may act out stories for themselves or other classes with improvised dialogue as you narrate. You may use the stories suggested in the units or use the children's own stories. A few simple props or hats add interest. Some headband patterns with animal ears are included in *The Arts—Circus* theme. Parents may be invited to see these informal drama experiences, as their presence alone is a reward to the child.

Students can work on inflection, stress, intonation, fluency, articulation carryover, and language structre in an active communicative situation through this approach. Other kinds of oral communication activities are suggested in each unit for individual or group practice.

Task cards

(Illustration note: SCRAPBOOK / MASKS / Think of all the different types of masks and give their uses....)

PROCEDURE FOR USING THE PROGRAM
(Sample Unit: Transportation—Space)

Getting Ready

1. Prepare a mural and/or cutouts and put up other suggested materials for the visual environment.

2. Take out the display box with objects to be used and set up the tactile display. Make task cards to go with it if appropriate.

3. Pull your file of pictures, project ideas, stickers, etc. relating to *Transportation—Space* and select activities which are applicable to your short-term objectives.

4. Prepare the home letters for distribution to the parents. Write comments on individual letters if necessary.

5. Make vocabulary cards on index card strips for skills practice.

6. Draw from the vocabulary lists and skills lists in this book the *Transportation—Space* items you will need for teaching or reinforcing particular skills with individuals or groups. Make up additional practice exercises if needed.

7. Check other units under those skill areas and *Language Remediation and Expansion: 100 Skill-Building Reference Lists* for additional material.

Think about transportation and space in light of curriculum goals or individual lesson plans and short-term objectives. For example, the speech-language pathologist may use the *Transportation—Space* unit for students working on:

1. articulation modification. Use words with the target sound from the vocabulary list for practice exercises.

2. articulation, voice, and fluency carryover. Use activities in the "Production of Language" section.

3. auditory discrimination. Use display articles and the mural in exercises on beginning sounds, sound blending, rhyming, etc.

4. morphology and syntax. Use scrambled sentences and the question game. Show transportation pictures to students in order to elicit verb or pronoun forms (for example, "The *man is driving* the car." "*He drove* the car."). Use *ride, fly, go, bring, come, leave, shut, sit, stand.*

5. semantics. Use homonyms, antonyms, compound words, incomplete sentences and words from the vocabulary list in the *Transportation—Space* unit. Also discuss the visual environment and items in the display.

6. cognitive tasks. Use analogies, classifying, associations, inferences, part-whole relationships, similarities-differences.

7. auditory sequencing. Use logical sentences, scrambled sentence sequence, scrambled word order, and following directions.

8. basic concepts. Use discussion of visual environment and manipulate and talk about objects in the display. Use the reproducible sheets for following directions.

9. verbal and nonverbal communication. Use activities under "Production of Language" and verbal activities under "Cognitive Tasks."

Introducing the Theme

As the students come in, play a space–sounds record, such as "The Planets" by Tomita (see Books and Phonograph Records List for the unit). Introduce the theme: "We will be thinking and talking about transportation and space during the next two weeks. Tell me what you see up here in space." Elaborate on the students' description of the visual environment. Invite them to bring in space or transportation items to share. Tell them what is in the parent letter — about the home projects. Perhaps read from a book about space or transportation.

Once you have "turned on" the students' thinking about the topic, move into the skills work, whether it be basic concepts, articulation. modification, vocabulary development and comprehension, or verbal expression. Setting the stage captures student interest and builds motivation. It also encourages convergent and divergent thinking and concept formation. The themes give continuity and cohesiveness to the sequence of tasks you set up because the students can relate information and use language in meaningful situations.

You will find that once you have started using the unit framework, you will think of many creative ideas and ways of adapting the theme to your therapy or classroom needs. The units are primarily set up for the remediation and expansion of language and communication skills. But the teacher of a self–contained class may easily extend the theme to math, social studies, spelling, art, and other subjects. The opportunity is there to interrelate information and concepts in many ways, thereby increasing retention of the material to be learned.

GENERALIZATION

Because using and studying language in contextual situations is interesting, stimulating, and meaningful, students become observant and adventurous about language. We have found that learning generalizes into other areas because of the interest buildup. Students are eager to report information they have learned at home. For example, in our *Food–Farm–Stores–Money* unit, the families had made mini-field trips to the grocery store to look for unusual foods. Robbie, a very quiet child, reported the next day, "My dad said when we were in Viet Nam we ate some monkey meat." The other children immediately questioned him, "How did it taste?", "Where did you find it?" and Robbie proudly answered.

In a brainstorming activity in the *Transportation–Space* theme, Sean added the word *houseboat* to the list and immediately said, "Hey, that's a compound word. Let's make a picture of it." We had previously talked about compound words and illustrated them. Other students delight in finding homonyms or rhyming words and want to make sentences using them. In the *Weather–Seasons–Time–Measurement* unit, we were talking about forms of precipitation and mentioned "icicle." Angie observed, "That rhymes with bicycle. There's an *icicle* on my *bicycle*."

Again, in the *Foods–Farm–Stores–Money* unit, we discussed how oranges grow. David eagerly offered, "I know what the parts of an orange are: *skin, seeds* and *juice* (relationships)." Juan added, "We have *skins* too (multiple meanings). It's the same word!" Communication skills really come alive!

PART II

Thematic Units

Outline of Sections and Activities

I. Concepts

II. Visual Environment

III. Displays

IV. Materials

V. Activities for Learning Concepts and Listening

VI. Home Projects and Field Trips

VII. Parent Letter

VIII. Books and Phonograph Records

IX. Skills Lists
   A. Phonology, Morphology, Syntax
      1. Articulation and Grammar Practice
      2. Irregular Verbs
      3. Auditory Discrimination
      4. Rhyming Sentences
      5. Scrambled Sentences
      6. Sentence Types
      7. Question Game

   B. Semantics
      1. Homonyms
      2. Antonyms
      3. Compound Words
      4. Adjectives and Adverbs
      5. Basic Concepts and Following Directions
      6. Idioms, Proverbs and Similes
      7. Scrambled Sentence Sequence
      8. Incomplete Sentences

   C. Cognitive Tasks
      1. Analogies
      2. Classification
      3. Categories
      4. Part–Whole Relationships
      5. Associations
      6. Similarities–Differences
      7. Inferences
      8. Logical Sequences

   D. Production of Language
      1. Nonverbal
      2. Production of Sentences
      3. Descriptions
      4. Storytelling
      5. Short Talks
      6. Improvisations
      7. Questions and Discussion Topics

X. Vocabulary Lists

XI. Story Shape

NOTE: Not all activities are in every unit. Additional activities are included where appropriate.

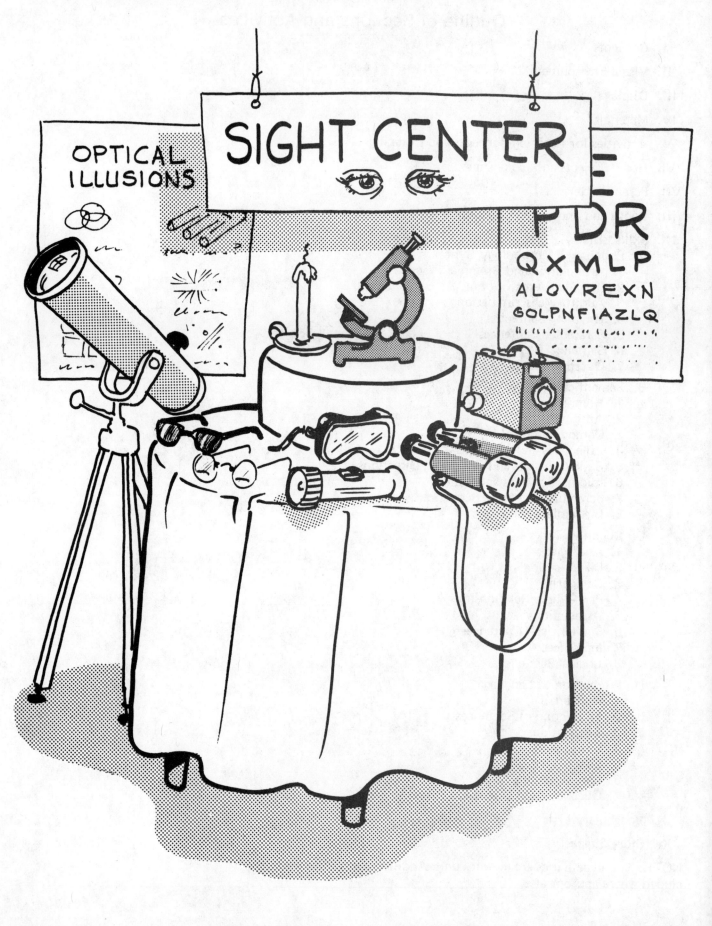

UNIT 1
Self—Senses—Emotions—Clothing

CONCEPTS

Each unit encompasses several related concept areas which may be explored, extended and adjusted to the age and interest level of the students. The basic concepts in Unit 1 are (1) history and knowledge of self, (2) care of self, (3) senses, (4) emotions, and (5) clothing.

VISUAL ENVIRONMENT

- *Five Senses* bulletin board set (Trend)
- *Your Body* posters (Instructor Publications)
- Large Halloween skeleton
- Sign Language Chart
- Pictures of people with different facial expressions
- *Body Parts Cards* (Communication Skill Builders)
- Add other materials you may have.
-
-
-
-
-
-
-
-
-

DISPLAYS

Different kinds of "hands-on" displays relating to the theme may be set up. Talk about the items, compare them, categorize, discuss functions, who uses them, when they are used, and how they work. Make up riddles, describe the objects in detail, tell a story about one and act it out. Make up task cards relating to the items to go with the display.

Sight Display

magnifying glass	mirror
eye glasses	a model of the eye
camera	goggles
contact lenses	optical illusions
vision chart	sample of Braille
microscope	telescope
kaleidoscope	candles
flashlight	

Body Care Display

bandages	tongue depressor
sling	splint
tape	eye dropper
X-rays	teeth X-rays
stethoscope	hot water bottle
heating pad	casts

Other Displays

Taste   Smell   Hearing   Touch
Collect other appropriate items.

MATERIALS

- Large child dolls with clothes (Peabody Language Development Kit — Level K)
- Large facial expression cards (GOAL — Milton Bradley)
- Small picture cards — family (GOAL — Milton Bradley)
- *Auditory Familiar Sounds* — tape and cards (Developmental Learning Materials)
- All kinds of musical instruments and noisemakers
- **Sound Boxes.** Use half-pint milk cartons or small boxes. Paint or cover the outsides with contact paper. Put a different object inside each box (cotton ball, large rock, marbles, coins, rubber bands, sticks, blocks, cereal, rice, salt, water). Students shake each box to determine its contents. You may make two of each and have the students listen for matching pairs.
- **Feel Box.** Cover or paint a cardboard box 12″ square or larger. Cut a hole in the side for a child's hand to fit through. Put objects of different textures, shapes and sizes in the box (wooden block, glove, ball, toy car, toothbrush, comb, small cup, candle, yoyo, balloon, necklace, baby rattle, etc.). The child puts his hand in, feels one object, and describes it for others to guess. Use a clue chart to help the child expand his verbal description. Include these concepts: *shape, parts, size, made of, used for, feels like.*
- **Materials Match.** Mount identical pieces of fabric on two 2″ x 2″ squares of tagboard. The child matches the like fabrics. Use stripes, plaids, checks, polka dots, fur, nylon, velvet, wool, felt, leather, cotton, lace, silk, knit, woven, crocheted fabrics. As you identify and discuss, look at the children's clothes for similar materials.
- *Perceive and Respond: Sounds Related to Body Functions* — tapes (Modern Education Corporation)
- Braille alphabet cards (These may be available from the local society for the blind or the American Printing House for the Blind, 1839 Frankfort Avenue, Louisville, Kentucky 40206.)
- Sequential Cards: *Health and Safety* (Developmental Learning Materials)
- Other materials you have.

Materials match.

ACTIVITIES FOR LEARNING CONCEPTS AND LISTENING

School photo

Paper body

- Play "Simon Says," telling children to touch their ears, wrist, thigh, and other body parts. Let the children give directions also.
- Make "touch" charts. Children attach items that have different textures such as foil, cotton, sandpaper, fur, plastic, rubber, wood, styrofoam, etc. Label each and talk about where they come from, how they are made, how they feel.
- Make paper cup puppets or finger puppets with the child's photograph (see illustration). The child may tell all about himself through the puppet ("I am eight years old. I like to play cars. There are five people in my family.") Make one of yourself and have conversations with the student.
- Use noisemakers for sequence games. The students close their eyes and guess the ones you played. They may then try to repeat the sequence.
- Make fingerprints and footprints.
- Use nursery rhymes which involve self and emotions: "Georgie Porgie," "Little Jack Horner," "Three Little Kittens," "Jack and Jill." Sing "Here We Go Round the Mulberry Bush," with the actions.
- Dance and sing the "Hokey Pokey."
- Make paper movies about "Self." Cut out or draw pictures and and glue on long strips of paper. Roll the movie through a shoebox screen and have the child narrate his story. Invite the parents in to share them.
- Make "ME" books to be finished at home with parent help. Pages may include:

  > This is a picture of me . . .
  > This is my hand (draw around it) . . .
  > I like to eat . . . I don't like to eat . . .
  > My best friend is . . . We like to play . . .
  > I am happy when . . . I am sad when . . .
  > I live at . . .
  > Someday I want to be a . . .

  The students may draw pictures to illustrate their responses. Share the books and place them in a "Young Authors" corner. Have older students dictate their own biographies while you print or type them.
- Print words from the vocabulary lists on small cards and have the students take turns acting out the words. Pictures may also be used on the cards.
- Use the skeleton in the visual environment for teaching body parts and following directions games.
- Visit the nurse's office. Ask her to talk about care of the body, show the first aid kit, etc.
- Brainstorm with the children and make lists of:

  > noises we make (gurgle, whisper, yell)
  > how things taste (sour, sweet, syrupy)
  > things we do with our fingers (snap, pinch, point).
- See section on categories for more suggestions.

The shoe box theatre...

THIS IS A PICTURE OF ME...

I AM ___ YEARS OLD.

The Big
Home Taste Test

HOME PROJECTS AND FIELD TRIPS

- *Take a Night Walk:* Listen for sounds outdoors and talk about them. What do you smell and see?

- *Have a Taste Test:* Cut several foods into small pieces. Blindfold the child and let him taste and identify the foods. Use peanut butter, apple, carrot, salt, sugar, honey, etc. Discuss how they taste (crunchy, sweet, sour, etc.).

- *Make Smell Books:* Staple five or six index cards together to make a small book. Have your child put a small amount of glue on each page and a small portion of a spice or other fragrant item (cocoa, chili powder, instant coffee, cinnamon, or vanilla on a cotton ball). Write the name on the reverse side of the card. Talk about how the substances smell and where they originate. Give a test to family members or friends. Let them smell each page and name the substances.

- Finish the "ME" book and have your child return it to school for sharing.

- Look at your child's baby book or family photo album with him. Talk about your child's history.

- Teach body parts to your child as you play games (for example, "Simon Says") or during bathtime.

- Look through magazines with your child and have him find and name body parts and emotions in the people pictures. This is a good "waiting game" for the doctor's office, etc.

- Play charades: Act out words on the vocabulary list included with the home letter.

- Practice nursery rhymes with your child.

SAMPLE LETTER

Dear Parents:

Our language theme for the next two weeks will be Self-Senses-Emotions-Clothing. We will be talking about, reading about and thinking about many aspects of this theme. Please help your child expand vocabulary and concepts by doing these activities:

HOME PROJECTS

1. Look at and talk about your child's baby book or your family picture album, recalling events in family life.

2. Help your child fill out the "ME" book and bring it back to school to share. Encourage your child to do most of the drawing and writing with your help.

3. Sit outdoors with your child for 5 or 10 minutes some evening. Listen very carefully and identify all the sounds you hear. Talk about them.

4. Make a list of all the things you can do with your fingers (scratch, pinch, point, etc.). The whole family can brainstorm words together. Explain the meanings of unfamiliar words and demonstrate them. Send the list to school.

5. Play "Simon Says," naming different body parts and things to do. (See vocabulary list below.)
   "Simon Says - touch your nose."
   "Simon Says - look sad."
   "Simon Says - touch your scalp."
   Let your child take turns giving directions for you to follow.

VOCABULARY. Use new words as often as you can and explain their meanings.

   Body Parts: wrist, waist, ankle, shoulder, cheek, thigh, heel, eyelid, elbow, jaw, throat, forehead, knuckles, ribs, collarbone, lungs (where are they)?

   Emotions: sad, lazy, bored, angry, surprised, nervous, frightened, excited, impatient, worried, proud, confused, peaceful, mean (act them out!)

<u>Eyes</u>: blink, squint, peek, stare, wink, peer (Show me!)

<u>Mouth</u>: scream, grin, whisper, smile, wheeze, babble, etc.

DINNER TABLE FAMILY DISCUSSION STARTERS (or for in the car or anywhere!)

1. What makes you mad, happy, excited?

2. Why do we dream? Tell about the craziest dream you ever had.

3. Why do we perspire? How does the water come out?

Expand on these subjects and think of others. Thank you for your help.

Sincerely,

BOOKS AND PHONOGRAPH RECORDS

Books

The Touch Me Book by Pat and Eve Witte (Golden Press).

Look Around and Listen by Jay Friedman (Grossett and Dunlap).

The Temper Tantrum Book by Edna Preston (Scholastic Book Services).

Sesame Street *How To Be A Grouch* by Caroll Spinney (Western Publishing Company).

Hop, Skip and Jump Book by Jack Kent (Random House).

Teeth. Hair. Sleep. Eyes. Clothes. Wonder Starter Books (Wonder Books).

Just For You by Mercer Mayer (Golden Press).

Just Me and My Dad by Mercer Mayer (Golden Press).

The Best Word Book Ever by Richard Scarry (Golden Press). This book has pictures in categories including body parts, actions, emotions, and clothes.

Charlie Brown's Super Book of Questions and Answers: about all kinds of animals . . . from snails to people! (Random House).

Any Mother Goose Nursery Rhyme book.

Traditional stories concerning emotions, self, and clothes: *The Ugly Duckling, Dumbo, Little Red Riding Hood, The Emperor's New Clothes, Cinderella.*

Phonograph Records

Sesame Street 2. Songs about the body and senses such as "Mad!", "Grouch Song," "I'm Pretty," "Everybody Wash," "Everyone Makes Mistakes" (Warner Brothers).

Hokey Pokey.

Mary Poppins, "I Love to Laugh" (Buena Vista Records).

Let Your Feelings Show: "Sad," "Fear," "Happy," "Grouchy" (Sesame Street).

Fair is Fair: "I'm a Person," "I Like You, You Like Me," "Talk To Me Nice," "The 'No' Song" (Sesame Street).

For complete book, record and material references, see List of Publishers in Appendix B.

SKILLS LISTS

Phonology, Morphology, Syntax

- See vocabulary lists on pages 39–41. Use these words for syllabication, sound blending, sound discrimination, and rhyming practice.

- For articulation modification, words with the target sound from the lists may be used for word, phrase, or sentence practice. Other tasks under "Production of Language" (page 36) are useful for carryover practice in context.

- Words from the vocabulary lists may be selected for practicing correct grammatical forms. Pictures, objects, the visual environment set-up, or the children themselves may serve as visual stimuli for the sentences. For example, the students describe other students:

    Pronouns:
    He has blue eyes.
    She has green eyes.
    She is clapping.

    Plurals:
    Billy has nice *teeth*.
    Anita has socks on her *feet*.

    Verbs:
    John *is throwing* the ball.
    John *threw* the ball.

- Make an alphabetical dictionary of body movement words with the students. Have them listen for the beginning sounds:
    A — act, ache
    B — blink, bounce, box
    C — clench, clap, cry

- Print words from the vocabulary lists *Rhyming* column on small cards. The student picks a card, thinks of a rhyming word, and acts out both words. Other students guess the words and describe the student's actions in sentences.
    KNEE — BEE
    "Tom hurt his *knee.*"
    "The *bee* stung him."

    You may wish to write the phonograms on the card (BLINK — sink, wink, rink, stink).

- See other units for more activities in this category.

Rhyming Sentences

- Read the sentence, emphasizing the first italicized word and omitting the second. Students fill in the rhyming word. (For more, see LRE,* List 2.)

- Remind the students that all the sentences are associated with the theme.
    I have *skin* on my *chin.*
    The evening *breeze* made me *sneeze.*
    My fingers *click;* my tongue can *lick.*

Language Remediation and Expansion: 100 Skill-Building Reference Lists by Catharine S. Bush (Tucson, Arizona: Communication Skill Builders, Inc., 1979).

You can *hop* 'til I say *stop.*
Her voice was *weak* when she tried to *speak.*
Lucy tied a *bow* on her little *toe.*
I hurt my *thigh* and I started to *cry.*
Your mouth can *drink;* your eye can *wink.*
Please don't *tickle;* I'll give you a *nickel.*

Minibook

Scrambled Sentences: Word Order
(LRE, Lists 15 and 16)

- Either read the sentences aloud or print them on cards. Students should rearrange the words in the correct order.

  3 Words
  hurts my back
  scared was I
  good candy tastes
  hands your clap
  is ticklish mom

  4 Words
  blue eyes my are
  stare don't at me
  jump high I can
  her is voice soft
  glasses wear you do

- Have the students make up other sentences about themselves.

Sentence Types

- Have students make up sentences of each type (declarative, interrogative, imperative and exclamatory) on one subject for a mini-book. The students may read them, using inflection and expression indicated by the punctuation. Demonstrate reading the sentences first.

  Example:
  Teeth
  I have twenty teeth.   (declarative)
  Do you have any cavities?   (interrogative)
  A shark has huge teeth!   (exclamatory)
  Brush your teeth right now.   (imperative)

- Other subjects for mini-books: *mad, whistle, tickle, muscles,* and other words associated with the theme.

Question Game

- Print answers (see list below) on small cards. Use other words from the vocabulary lists. The student draws a card and must ask a question to elicit the answer from the other students. Make a list of question words (what, who, when, where, how). Tell the child which word to start with if he has difficulty with the task.

Who What Where When How

Answers	Questions
at night	(*When* do you sleep?)
kick it	
fingerprints	
around your waist	(*Where* do you wear your belt?)
a hearing aid	

cry a lot	(*What* do babies do?)
eyelashes	
sour	(*How* do lemons taste?)
to help them see better	(*Why* do people wear glasses?)

- Variation: Show an answer card to the group. Each student must ask a *different* question to elicit that answer.

Semantics

Homonyms (LRE, Lists 23–26)

- Select homonyms from the vocabulary list (pages 39–41). Discuss the word pairs. Have the students make up sentences using both the words. For example: "The sore on my *heel* will not *heal.*"

- The students may act out the word pairs.

Antonyms (LRE, Lists 28–30)

- Match the antonym pairs on sets of cards or lists.

- Have the students use both words in one sentence to illustrate the meanings: "Sugar tastes *sweet* but lemon tastes *sour.*"

- Students may act out the pairs and other students guess the words. Demonstrate frequently for the students.

Senses:	**Body:**
sweet–sour	up–down (arms)
hot–cold	out–in (tongue)
light–dark	left–right
loud–soft	strong–weak
light–heavy	asleep–awake
fancy–plain	laugh–cry
curly–straight	whisper–yell

Emotions:	
happy–sad	proud–ashamed
brave–scared	worried–relieved
calm–nervous	polite–rude
interested–bored	sick–well
depressed–joyful	young–old
timid–aggressive	hungry–full

Compound Words (LRE, Lists 21–22)

- Select words from the vocabulary lists. Say the first half of a compound word. A student completes the word and uses it in a sentence.

- Students may illustrate the two word parts on a card and print the word on the back. Other students decode the words.

- Students may write stories using as many of the compound words in this theme as they can. As they read the stories to the other students, they leave out the compound words and the class tries to fill them in.

Adjectives and Adverbs (LRE, Lists 31–33)

- On small cards, print the names of body parts. Have the students think up *adjectives* to describe each part.

hard, white	teeth
red, pretty	lips
bony, smooth	knees

- Print actions on cards. Students think of *adverbs* to describe **each.** They can act out their word pairs.

smiles	*nervously*
talks	*softly*
winks	*mischievously*

- Students may also describe pictures of people showing different emotions.

Basic Concepts and Following Directions
(LRE, Lists 19–20; 47–49)

- Play "Simon Says" using body parts and actions in the directions.

- Use the skeleton ditto sheet (page 32). Give directions to be followed by the students.

    "Put a red X on his toe."
    "Draw a circle around his elbow."

- Use the visual environment and display for following directions. Let each child take a turn following and giving directions.

    "Point to the laughing face."
    "Pick up the object you take pictures with."
    "Show me the skeleton's elbow; then touch your knee."

Increase complexity of the directions as the students improve.

Idioms, Proverbs and Similes (LRE, Lists 36–39)

- Discuss the meanings of *idioms* related to the theme. The students may illustrate them or use them in stories.

shoot off your mouth	hard-hearted
frog in my throat	get off my back
blue in the face	foot in the door
I'm all ears	turn up your nose
slip of the tongue	pick your brains
Others:	

Scrambled Sentence Sequence (LRE, Lists 41–42)

- Print the sentences on index card strips. The student should arrange them in the proper order. You may also cut the strips into word and/or phrase units. The student arranges words into sentences and then sentences in sequence.

Bill saw a skeleton.	2
Bill went into a haunted house.	1
He got scared and ran home.	3
I bought some ice cream.	1
My stomach got very cold.	3
I ate all of it.	2
Susie had a toothache.	1
She went to the dentist.	2
He pulled her tooth.	3

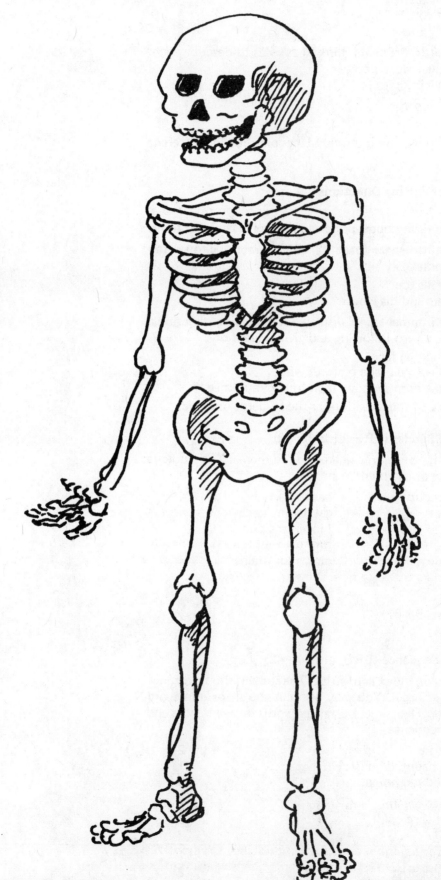

    Copyright© 1980 by Communication Skill Builders, Inc.

He hurt his knee.	2
Albert fell off his bike.	1
He started crying.	3
Felice put on her raincoat.	2
It was raining.	1
She went outside to play.	3

- Have the students make up more sequences using words from the vocabulary lists.

- The sentences may be presented verbally for a more difficult activity.

Incomplete Sentences (LRE, Lists 43–46)

- Read the sentence and ask the student to say any appropriate word for the missing word. Encourage divergent responses.

- You may point to the initial letter on an alphabet strip as a clue. The students may create new sentences with new vocabulary words in the unit.

Billy has a soft v_____ .

Can you w_____ your eye?

Don't s_____ so loud!

That food s_____ delicious.

I fell down and broke my l____ .

The swimmer wears g_____ on his eyes.

How much do you w_____?

Nancy sewed the s_____ on her dress.

What kind of s_____ do you like to wear?

Cognitive Tasks

- The following exercises make good family word games. Send a set home occasionally for the student to try out with his family. The families can also help make up new items related to the theme.

Analogies (LRE, Lists 52–62)

Finger is to *hand* as *toe* is to _____ .	foot
Nose is to *sneeze* as *mouth* is to _____ .	cough
Foot is to *height* as *pound* is to _____ .	weight
Frown is to *mad* as *smile* is to _____ .	happy
Microscope is to *eyes* as *stethoscope* is to _____ .	ears
See is to *saw* as *run* is to _____ .	ran
Tooth is to *teeth* as *foot* is to _____ .	feet
Necklace is to *neck* as *bracelet* is to _____ .	wrist
Pinch is to *fingers* as *kick* is to _____ .	foot
Lung is to *air* as *stomach* is to _____ .	food

- See *Language Remediation and Expansion: 100 Skill-Building Reference Lists* (Lists 52–62) for more comprehensive instructions for teaching analogies.

Classification (LRE, Lists 65-68)

- The student tells which three words go together and why. Mix up the words in the oral presentation.

pinch, draw, snap	kick
thigh, calf, ankle	wrist
telescope, binoculars, microscope	telephone
lungs, stomach, intestines	knee
angry, mad, irritated	cheerful
bracelet, ring, watch	glove
sing, yell, talk	whisper
tall, huge, gigantic	small
seam, zipper, collar	shirt
boots, sandals, shoes	slippers

Categories (LRE, Lists 63-64)

- Brainstorm items in categories on the theme. Make lists, collages, mobiles or card sets to use for other activities.

    Things you do with your feet
    Things you look through
    Things inside your body
    Things that make you mad
    Things you wear on your eyes
    Things that taste sweet
    Kinds of illnesses
    Ways voices sound
    Things you have two of on your body

- Make a chart with the letters of the child's name across the top. Down the left side, list the following categories: things I do, I have, I want, I eat, I play. The student fills in the appropriate words beginning with each letter as a class activity or home project with the family.

	J	A	M	E	S
I am...					
I can...	jump				spell
I like		Amy	Mopeds		
I eat...	jam		milk		soup
I play...			marbles		soccer

Part-Whole Relationships (LRE, Lists 69-70)

- Read the sentence, leaving out the last word. The student fills in the missing word. Then have him name other parts of the whole. For example: shoe — sole, heel, lace

- Make up new sentences using vocabulary list items.

A *tongue* is part of the _____ (mouth/shoe) _____ .

A *sleeve* is part of a _____ (shirt/coat) _____ .

A *fingernail* is part of your _____ (finger) _____ .

Your *scalp* is part of your _____ (head) _____ .

A *lens* is part of the _____ (eye/camera) _____ .

A *mask* is part of a _____ (costume) _____ .

The *spine* is part of the _____ (back) _____ .

A *hem* is part of a _____ (dress/shirt) _____ .

The *shin* is part of your _____ (leg) _____ .

Associations (LRE, Lists 71-73)

- Brainstorm all the words that would be associated with one subject on the theme. Encourage divergent responses. Ask the students why the words are associated. For instance:

Sleep

eyes	night	dream	alarm clock
bed	tired	nap	bedtime story
yawn	blanket	crib	nightmare
dark	awake	snore	

List the words on a chart or on the story shape included in the unit. Then have the students tell a story using as many of these words as possible. Tape record, type or print it. Individual or group stories may be told.

- Put a subject on the chalkboard each day and let the students list associated words. You might do this in teams for an interesting group activity.

- Other words on the theme for associations: *whisper, fingerprints, barefoot, embarrassed.*

Similarities-Differences (LRE, Lists 74-76)

- Have the students tell all the ways the items are alike and then how they are different. Use a clue chart to assist: size, shape, use, location (where it is found), color, parts, texture, sound, category, action, feeling.

elbow-knee	cough-sneeze
grin-smile	jog-skip
glasses-goggles	child-adult
shy-afraid	stare-peek
eyebrow-eyelashes	shirt-coat
Other:	

- Have the students compare objects in the display.

Inferences (LRE, Lists 78-79)

- Read the first general clue. Elicit from the students as many appropriate responses as possible. Then read the second clue. Encourage the students to combine information before guessing. Read the third clue.

I am below the waist. You can bend me. I have a nail on me.	toe
You do this in a game. You need a ball to do it. Sometimes the ball goes over a goalpost.	kick
I am usually black and white. Each person has a different one. I am usually made at the police station.	fingerprint
I am something you do with your fingers. Your fingers go back and forth. You do this when you itch.	scratch
You wear me. I am worn mostly in the summer. You usually get wet when you wear me.	swimsuit

- Remind the students that the answer will relate to the theme. Have the students make up their own clue sets.

Production of Language

Nonverbal (LRE, Lists 81-86)

- Act out words from the vocabulary lists. Use opposites, idioms, scrambled sequences and homonyms. Make up sets of word cards for repeated use.

Descriptions

- Use the Feel Box (see "Materials" section). Students describe objects using specific information. They may also describe items in the display.

Storytelling (LRE, List 90)

- After the theme has been presented and discussed, have the student dictate a story relating to the theme. Print it on the construction paper story shape. The shape pattern is at the end of the unit.

- Suggested subjects for Self unit stories:
  My Scary Dream
  The Happiest Day of My Life
  When I Was a Baby

- Tell the students a story. Help them make flannel board characters which can be used by students to practice storytelling. Students may then present their stories to a small group of peers or younger children.

- Paper cup puppets or pictures may also be used as visual aides.

- Some good stories that deal with the theme of self, senses, emotions and clothes are: *The Ugly Duckling, Dumbo, The Boy Who Cried Wolf, Jack and the Beanstalk, The Emperor's New Clothes,*

Cinderella and *Red Riding Hood.* These can also be used for creative drama. The students improvise dialogue as they act out the story. You may wish to narrate the story to keep the action going.

Short Talks (LRE, Lists 91–95)

■ These are useful for articulation carryover and evaluation of speech and language production. Record the talks, play them back, and evaluate them with the students. Suggested topics are:

> My Life History
> The Invention of Braille
> How To Take Fingerprints
> How the Heart Works (Eyes See, etc.)
> What Really Makes Me Mad
> The Scariest Thing I've Ever Done
> Describe another student's face. Others in the group may draw it.
> Give a commercial for a toothpaste that lasts forever.
> Give a commercial for shoes that make you weightless.
> Invent and tell about clothes to wear in the year 2002.

Improvisations (LRE, Lists 87 and 96)

■ These can be done individually or in small groups; they may be nonverbal or verbal presentations.

> You pick a beautiful red apple from a tree. Take a bite. It has a worm in it.
>
> You get a big present for your birthday. You unwrap it and find out it's something you already have.
>
> You get into a very crowded elevator. All of a sudden you have to sneeze. Show what happens.
>
> Go to a clothing store. Try on some clothes. Show us what you think about them.
>
> You are studying. You smell something. Go and investigate. Let us know what it is.

Questions and Discussion Topics

■ As children become involved in the ideas and concepts of a particular unit and become more motivated to seek related information, they ask questions. Print their questions on paper strips and display them. Have the students speculate as to the answers. Help them find information. Reinforce their curiosity! Offer other questions for problem-solving.

■ In this unit, students might want to know:

> Why doesn't it hurt to cut my fingernails?
> Why do I yawn?
> What happens when I sneeze?
> Why do my teeth fall out?
> Why does my stomach growl?
> What makes me itch?

■ These questions may be suggested in the home letter as dinner table discussion topics. The students may bring to school their answers and other questions their families have discussed. Share these with the group.

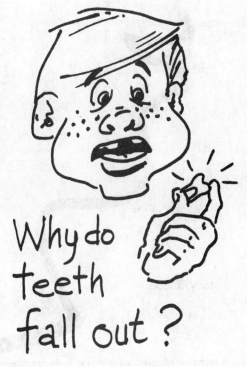

Why do teeth fall out?

Story Shape

VOCABULARY LIST

WORD	Rhyme	Compound	Homonym	Syllables	Phonemes
Parts of the Body					
wrist	✓			1	4
waist (waste)	✓		✓	1	4
ankle				2	4
shoulder				2	
cheek	✓			1	3
chin	✓			1	3
elbow				2	4
jaw	✓			1	2
throat	✓			1	4
forehead		✓		2	
eyebrow		✓		2	
eyelash		✓		2	
brain	✓			1	4
tongue	✓			1	3
lips	✓			1	4
teeth				1	3
arm	✓			1	
leg				1	3
knee	✓			1	2
heel (heal)	✓		✓	1	3
toe (tow)	✓		✓	1	2
fingernail		✓		4	
skull				1	4
collarbone		✓		3	
chest			✓	1	4
ribs				1	4
lung				1	3
spine	✓			1	4
nostril				2	
thigh	✓			1	2
calf			✓	1	3
shin	✓			1	3
palm			✓	1	4
sole (soul)	✓		✓	1	3
stomach				2	
knuckle				2	4
pupil			✓	2	
palate (palette)			✓	2	
heart	✓			1	4
skin	✓			1	4
eardrum		✓		2	

WORD	Rhyme	Compound	Homonym	Syllables	Phonemes
muscle (mussel)			✓	2	4
heartbeat		✓		2	
freckle				2	
scalp			✓	1	
windpipe		✓		2	
breathe				1	4
vein (vain, vane)	✓		✓	1	3
tonsil				2	
blood				1	4
Eyes					
peek (peak)	✓		✓	1	3
peer (pier)	✓		✓	1	3
squint				1	
wink	✓			1	4
stare (stair)	✓		✓	1	4
blink	✓			1	
watch			✓	1	3
look	✓			1	3
glance				1	
open				1	4
glare	✓			1	4
blind			✓	1	
glasses			✓	2	
spectacles				3	
goggles				2	
binoculars				4	
telescope				3	
microscope				3	
Mouth					
cough				1	3
sneeze	✓			1	4
eat	✓			1	2
chew	✓			1	2
swallow			✓	2	
kiss				1	3
grin	✓			1	4
yawn				1	3
whistle				2	4
talk	✓			1	3
scream	✓			1	

VOCABULARY LIST

WORD	Rhyme	Compound	Homonym	Syllables	Phonemes
Mouth (continued)					
babble				2	4
whisper				2	
cry	✓			1	3
sob	✓			1	3
yell	✓			1	3
taste	✓			1	4
lick	✓			1	3
wheeze	✓			1	4
Fingers/Hands					
scratch				1	
pinch				1	4
point			✓	1	4
grab	✓			1	4
pick	✓		✓	1	3
wiggle				2	4
clap	✓			1	4
rub	✓			1	3
strum	✓			1	
wave	✓		✓	1	3
slap	✓			1	4
tap	✓			1	3
pound	✓		✓	1	4
snap	✓		✓	1	4
shake	✓		✓	1	3
pull				1	3
push				1	3
bend	✓			1	4
Miscellaneous					
headache		✓		2	
barefoot		✓		2	
fingerprint		✓		3	
Feelings					
afraid				2	
angry				2	
amazed				2	
bored (board)	✓		✓	1	4
brave	✓			1	4
cold	✓			1	4

WORD	Rhyme	Compound	Homonym	Syllables	Phonemes
curious				3	
confused				2	
disappointed				4	
doubtful				2	
envious				3	
embarrassed				3	
exhausted				3	
friendly				2	
foolish				2	
hungry				2	
ill	✓			1	2
innocent				3	
lonely				2	
mad	✓			1	3
happy				2	
proud	✓			1	4
sleepy				2	
shocked				1	4
silly				2	4
strong	✓			1	
tense			✓	1	4
timid				2	
uptight				2	
victorious				4	
wicked				2	
weak (week)	✓		✓	1	3
Clothing					
shoelace		✓		2	
waistband		✓		2	
raincoat		✓		2	
sweatshirt		✓		2	
earmuffs		✓		2	
cape				1	3
mitten				2	
glove				1	4
cap	✓			1	3
scarf				1	
shirt				1	3
pants			✓	1	
belt	✓			1	3
shorts				1	

VOCABULARY LIST

WORD	Rhyme	Compound	Homonym	Syllables	Phonemes
Clothing (continued)					
sock	✓		✓	1	3
ring	✓		✓	1	3
muffler				2	
dress	✓		✓	1	4
diaper				2	4
shoe	✓			1	3
sandal				2	
slipper				2	
necklace		✓		2	
bracelet				2	
buckle				2	
Other					
height	✓			1	3
weight (wait)	✓		✓	1	3
age	✓			1	2

WORD	Rhyme	Compound	Homonym	Syllables	Phonemes
Add Students' Names					
John	✓			1	3
Lucy				2	4

UNIT 2
Family—Home—School

CONCEPTS

Unit 2 stresses families and family relationships, homes and customs, global awareness, school facilities and activities, and toys and games.

VISUAL ENVIRONMENT

- Cutouts of homes (pages 44 and 45)
- Neighborhood poster (Peabody Kit — Level K)
- Playground poster (GOAL — Milton Bradley)
- Aerial map of your city (may be available at city offices)
- United States map
- Mounted pictures of families from all over the world
-
-
-
-
-
-
-
-
-
-

DISPLAYS

- **Neighborhood Display:** Set up a model of a city with blocks for houses, and toy cars. The students may help you plan the city and create the display. The Play Family Village (Fisher-Price) is a fascinating, durable toy which makes a good learning center for manipulation and verbal stimulation.

- **Toy Display:** Collect toys of yesteryear and from other countries for students to try out and talk about. Students may bring some from home to share.

- **Homes Display:** If students make models of homes from "junk" as a home project, put these on display.

-

-

-

-

-

MATERIALS

- Family and household cards (GOAL — Milton Bradley)
- Mix-n-Match Go-Together puzzles (Trend)
- Motor Expressive cards (Developmental Learning Materials)
- Association cards (Developmental Learning Materials, Teaching Resources)
- **Go-Together Objects.** Make up a set of objects that go together (toothbrush-toothpaste, vase-flowers, salt-pepper, paper-envelope, coin-purse, washcloth-soap, lock-key, chair-table, flashlight-battery, etc.). Have the students find the sets and tell why the objects go together.
- **All Possible Uses.** Place in an interesting container (heart-shaped candy box, plastic pumpkin, fancy basket) some common household objects such as a sponge, a rubber band, a table knife, or a paper cup. Ask the students to think of all the possible uses of the object you take out. Encourage divergent responses.
- Globe and maps
- Toy telephones
- *Perceive and Respond: Sounds Around the House* — tape (Modern Education Corporation)
- Wipe-Off Association Cards — Home (Trend)
- Classification By Use Cards (Learning Development Aids)
- Classification/Logical Order Cards — Buildings (Milton Bradley)
-
-
-
-
-
-
-
-

ACTIVITIES FOR LEARNING CONCEPTS AND LISTENING

- Talk about kinds of dwellings people live in. Refer to home cut-outs in the visual environment. Compare, contrast, describe, talk about the people who live in them, the locations, etc. Discuss the kinds of homes the students live in.

- Talk about neighborhoods and where the students live. Locate their homes on an aerial map or together draw a neighborhood map. Then discuss the city, state, country, continent, and finally the world, to help the child gain a sense of location in his social environment. Use maps and globes.

- Use play telephones to call friends and places in the neighborhood, such as the fire station, grocery store and library, to give or obtain information.

- Pantomime locations (LRE, List 86): beach, beauty shop, church, dentist's office, football stadium, cafeteria, ice cream parlor, nursery, pet shop, park, service station, shoe store, etc. Emphasize specific actions to convey information. Help the students visualize the environment.

- Brainstorm titles of relatives, such as cousin, grandfather or sister. List them on a chart. Talk about the students' families.

- Make models of imaginative dwellings out of "junk." The students may work on these at home with family help. Have the students explain the use of their invention to the others. Display the homes in the library or elsewhere at school.

- Talk about games and toys from other parts of the world. Encourage students to ask their families for help and bring in toys or games to try. Each student may give directions to other students for playing.

- Have the students practice these nursery rhymes that involve homes and school: "Peter, Peter, Pumpkin Eater," "The Old Woman Who Lived In the Shoe," "Mary Had a Little Lamb," "A Dillar, a Dollar, a Ten O'Clock Scholar," and the fingerplay, "Here Is the Church, Here Is the Steeple."

-

-

-

-

HOME PROJECTS AND FIELD TRIPS

- Fill out the "Family Tree" (page 48) at home. Talk about and find pictures of family members. Students may glue on photos or draw pictures with your help. Have your child take the Family Tree to school to share.

- Make a "Family Favorites" survey (see page 49). Help your child fill in the spaces. (At school: When the charts are returned to school, tally up one or two items and discuss the favorites. "Most of the people surveyed like football." "The favorite animal of the children is the cat.")

- Help your child draw a floor plan of your home. (At school: Display these in the classroom after discussing them. Encourage parents to use vocabulary words from your parent letter to expand concepts.)

- Take a neighborhood walk. The family can list all the businesses, parks and other interesting places and perhaps stop at one or two to find out some new information.

- Make a family "Body Poster" on a large sheet of butcher paper. Talk about the sizes and shapes. (At school: Draw around the child. The child can then draw around each family member, even the pets, on the same paper. Families are more likely to complete tasks if the materials are sent home. In the home letter, always encourage the families to send the projects back to school as soon as possible.)

- Invite the parents and families to school for a short "Family Night." Display the children's projects.

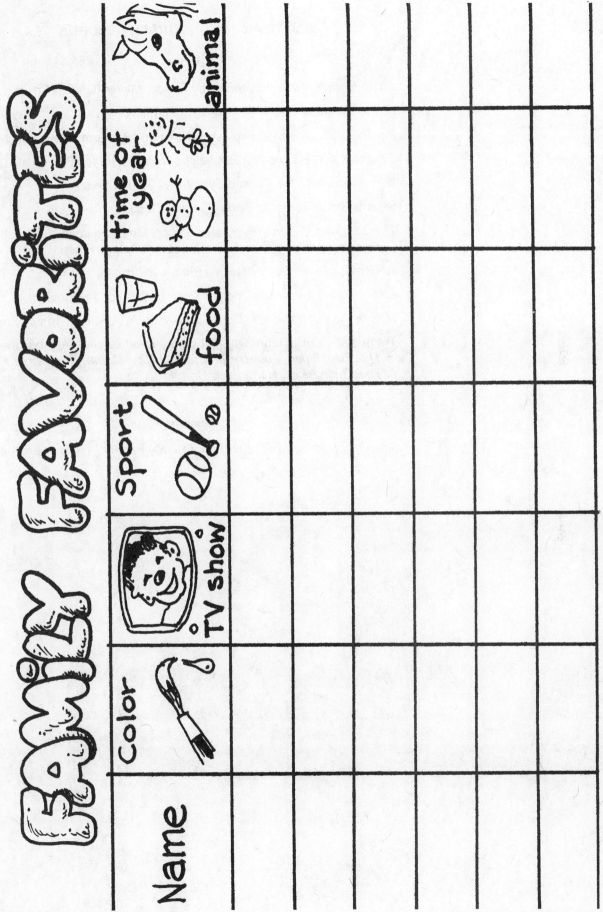

BOOKS AND PHONOGRAPH RECORDS

Books

Little Monster's Neighborhood by Mercer Mayer (Golden Press).

Homes. Wonder Books (Grosset and Dunlap).

Inside-Outside by Stan and Jan Berenstein (Random House).

Sesame Street *People In Your Neighborhood* (Golden Press).

Who Lives Here? by Pat and Eve Witte (Golden Press).

Sesame Street *Together Book* (Golden Press).

The Best Word Book Ever, sections on family members, household objects, and homes, by Richard Scarry (Golden Press).

All Kinds of Families by Norma Simon (Whitman).

Eliza's Daddy by Ianthe Thomas (Harcourt Brace Javonovich).

Winnie the Pooh and the Tight Squeeze by A. A. Milne (Golden Press).

Traditional stories concerning homes, families and neighborhoods: *The Pied Piper, Country Mouse and City Mouse, The Three Pigs, The Three Bears, Hansel and Gretel.*

Records

Sesame Street Record, "Five People In My Family" (Warner Brothers).

SKILLS LISTS
(Instructions for each exercise are given in Unit 1.)

Phonology, Morphology, Syntax

- Object Sets. Use the sets of small familiar objects (see Appendix A) for initial consonant or long and short vowel discrimination practice. Have the students say the names of objects, listen for the target sound, and place them in the correct baskets.

- For articulation practice, the student may select one or two objects from the target sound object set (s, r, sh, etc.) and make up a sentence about them.

  "The **s**eal **s**aw the **s**ign."
  "The **ch**icken **s**at on the **ch**ain."

Rhyming Sentences (LRE, List 2)

Johnny said *ouch* when he sat on the *couch*.

I lost my *ring* when I swung on the *swing*.

Will you *send* a gift to your *friend?*

The little *mouse* ran into his *house*.

Can we *rent* a camping *tent?*

Bill hid in the *tower* for almost an *hour*.

The old *slave* lived in a *cave*.

Ted said, "Put your *head* on the *bed*."

Your little *brother* looks like your *mother*.

We played in the *dark* at the neighborhood *park*.

Scrambled Sentences (LRE, Lists 15-16)

3 Words
the refrigerator open
friends have I
ghosts attic like
fun treehouses are
cries baby our

4 Words
townhouse your big is
dad my ball plays
state a is Texas
principal is nice our
castle is where the

Sentence Types

Castle
A castle is a big building.   (declarative)
Who lives in it?   (interrogative)
A giant lives there!   (exclamatory)
Be very quiet.   (imperative)

- Other subjects for mini-books: *recess, treehouse, caves, castle, babies.*

Question Game (See Unit I for directions.)

Answers	Questions
in the sink	(*Where* do you wash dishes?)
a fireplace	
grandfather	
an igloo	
in a haunted house	
the principal	
after school	
with my family	
hopscotch	
a castle	

- Select a set of objects (see Appendix A) or use the objects in the display. One student composes a question about an object. Another student answers the question. You may wish to select the question word to be used.

  "How many jacks are in the set?"
  "Which toy is made of wood and plastic?"
  "Where do you fly the model airplane?"

Semantics

Homonyms (LRE, Lists 23-26)

- See vocabulary list.

Antonyms (LRE, Lists 28-30)

mother–father	woman–man
adult–child	niece–nephew
enemy–friend	daughter–son
aunt–uncle	husband–wife
north–south	east–west
floor–ceiling	inside–outside
country–city	exterior–interior
private–public	front–back
vacant–occupied	big–small
length–width	

Compound Words (LRE, Lists 21-22)

- See vocabulary list.

Adjectives (LRE, List 31)

- Help the students think of adjectives to describe the homes in the visual environment.

  "The castle is *huge, gloomy* and *dark.*"

  Then tell a story about it. Students can take turns adding to the story when you point to them. They should use as many adjectives as they can.

  "It has *gigantic pointed* towers. A *fat, scary* monster lives inside."

Idioms, Proverbs and Similes (LRE, Lists 36-40)

paint the town red
on the house
hit the ceiling
take the floor
get out of bed on the wrong side
chip off the old block

The grass is always greener on the other side of the street.
People who live in glass houses shouldn't throw stones.
Like father, like son.
A friend in need is a friend indeed.

Others:

Scrambled Sentence Sequence (LRE, Lists 41-42)

Allen rang the doorbell.	1
He went inside the haunted house.	2
A ghost scared him.	3
The giant chased him.	3
Jack climbed the beanstalk.	1
He saw a castle.	2
She had a baby.	2
We named him Phil.	3
Mother went to the hospital.	1
We went out to recess.	2
The bell rang.	1
We played in the sandbox.	3
The Eskimos formed snow into blocks.	1
They built a fire inside.	3
They made an igloo.	2

- Make up more with the students.

Incomplete Sentences (LRE, Lists 43-46)

Somebody rang the b_____.

Get some wood for the f_____.

My u_____ is visiting us.

The Indians lived in t_____.

Jack saw the giant's c_____.

Take your b_____ to the library.

Our s_____ plays with dolls.

Anita d_____ on the chalkboard.

We stayed in a m_____ on our vacation.

What s_____ do you live on?

Cognitive Tasks

Analogies (LRE, Lists 52–62)

Boy is to *nephew* as *girl* is to _____. niece

Attic is to *high* as *cellar* is to _____. low

King is to *castle* as *ghost* is to _____. haunted house

Arizona is to *state* as *America* is to _____. country

School is to *study* as *park* is to _____. play

Stove is to *kitchen* as *shower* is to _____. bathroom

Houseboat is to *water* as *camper* is to _____. street

Yard is to *house* as *playground* is to _____. school

Baby is to *young* as *grandfather* is to _____. old

Teacher is to *classroom* as *principal* is to _____. office

Classification (LRE, Lists 65–68)

- Have the students think up additional sets using words from the vocabulary lists.

slide, swing, jungle gym	playground
footstool, bookcase, chair	bathtub
nephew, brother, father	aunt
basement, attic, porch	house
cafeteria, office, gymnasium	stadium
stove, refrigerator, sink	bed
grandmother, father, adult	baby
motel, hotel, condominium	cabin
carpet, sidewalk, rug	curtain

Categories (LRE, Lists 63–64)

Cities in your state
Things in your bathroom
Things on the playground
Places to live that are taller than one story
Names of students in your class
Names of streets
Indoor games
Things you can sit on
Kinds of buildings

- Make up more with the students.

Part-Whole Relationships (LRE, Lists 69–70)

A *dungeon* is part of a _____ (castle) .

Stairs are part of a _____ (house) .

A *cafeteria* is part of a _____ (school) .

A *sister* is part of a _____ (family) .

California is part of _____ (the United States) .

A *neighborhood* is part of the _____ (city) .

The *ceiling* is part of a _____ (room) .

A *lobby* is part of a _____ (hotel) .

The *shower* is part of the _____ (bathroom) .

Stripes are part of the _____ (flag) .

There can be several answers to some of these. Consider each response carefully.

Associations (LRE, Lists 71-73)

Flag — pole, red, white and blue, stripes, American, wave, parade, display, cloth, stars, 4th of July, salute, pledge.

Grandmother — kind, babysit, rocking chair, presents, grandfather, visit, knitting, relative, compound word.

- Other words for association: *principal, teenager, mansion, recess.*

Similarities-Differences (LRE, Lists 74-76)

map–globe	adult–teenager
playground–park	igloo–hogan
hotel–apartment	village–city
slide–swing	aunt–grandmother
tower–dungeon	bedroom–living room

- Other:

Inferences (LRE, Lists 78-79)

I am a kind of home.
I can be moved.
I have wheels.   mobile home

I am a person in the family.
I am not an adult.
I cry a lot.   baby

I am round.
You can find things on me.
I represent the earth.   globe

I am part of the school.
I hold a lot of people.
You eat here.   cafeteria

I am a game.
You run when you play me.
Someone has to be "it."   tag

- Give the students five words each. Let them make up their own three-clue riddles (teacher, flagpole, treehouse, lamp, mother).

Logical Sequences (LRE, List 80)

- Present a group of words in scrambled order. The students rearrange them in logical sequence. Start with only three items and then progress to more.

baby-child-teenager-adult-senior citizen	(age)
hut-cabin-townhouse-mansion-skyscraper	(size)
pillow-chair-bed-piano	(value)

```
neighborhood-city-county-state-country-
hemisphere                                    (location)
basement-ground floor-2nd floor-attic          (location)
cup-pail-bathtub-swimming pool                 (volume)
cushion-stool-chair-throne                     (size)
```

- Order objects or toys according to size, weight, value, speed. Use toy cars, balls, spoons, egg carton sections, animals, pencils, or other common objects.

- Other:

Production of Language

Nonverbal (LRE, Lists 81–86)

- Print the names of different kinds of homes on small cards. A student draws a card and pantomimes going into that home. Talk about size, shape, and parts of the home that can be shown through body language.

- Pantomime using some object at school or at home. The other students guess what the object is.

Production of Sentences (LRE, List 88)

- The student selects a card with three words on it. He or she then makes up a sentence using the words in any order. For example:

  baby-hospital-mother: "Mother brought the baby home from the hospital."

recess-slide-teacher	treehouse-cousins-visit
lamp-broke-table	cave-fire-cold
vacation-cabin-summer	park-friends-play
Eskimo-igloo-snow	refrigerator-eat-snack
family-cousins-visit	doorbell-telephone-dad

- Other:

Descriptions (LRE, List 89)

- Describe a member of your family.
- Describe some place in the school. The other students guess the location.
- Describe a kind of home.
- Describe your bedroom.
- Other:

Storytelling

- Act out one of these stories: *The Pied Piper, Country Mouse and the City Mouse, The Three Pigs, The Three Bears,* or *Hansel and Gretel.* First talk with the students about the kinds of homes involved and the characters. You may wish to use the headband patterns for making simple costumes (see pages 199–201).

- Video-tape their stories or present them informally for the parents or another class.

- Other:

Short Talks (LRE, Lists 91-95)

- Give directions to get to the flagpole, cafeteria, etc.
- Tell how to put up a tent.
- Tell all about Uncle Sam.
- Invent and tell about a house you could carry with you.
- Tell why you like your best friend.
- Give a commercial for a toy store.
- Bring your favorite toy and demonstrate how it works.
- Use a puppet and give a commercial for a new space toy.
- Tell why people should not pollute.
- Other:

Improvisations (LRE, Lists 87, 96)

- You are exploring and find a cave. You meet someone who lives there. Who is it? What happens?
- You borrow your dad's new watch. It breaks. Show us how you tell him.
- You are moving into a new house. You hear a strange noise in the attic. Investigate.
- It is your birthday. Your brother gives you a big present. You open it and find out it is something you already have.
- You are in the cafeteria. You get your favorite lunch. Someone bumps into you and it spills. Show what you do.
- Think up other situations to role-play.

VOCABULARY LIST

WORD	Rhyme	Compound	Homonym	Syllables	Phonemes
Relationships					
mother				2	4
father				2	4
sister				2	
brother				2	
uncle				2	4
aunt (ant)			✓	1	3
cousin				2	
grandmother		✓		3	
grandfather		✓		3	
relative				3	
niece				1	3
nephew				2	
stepfather		✓		3	
guardian				3	
ancestor				3	
heir (air)	✓		✓	1	2
child				1	4
adult				2	
teenager				3	
minor (miner)			✓	2	4
family				3	
neighbor				2	4
friend				1	
Boundaries					
neighborhood				3	
block		✓		1	
city				2	4
state	✓		✓	1	4
county				2	
country		✓		2	
suburb				2	
continent				3	
earth				1	2
hemisphere				3	
universe				3	
galaxy				3	
solar system				4	
map	✓			1	3
park	✓		✓	1	4

WORD	Rhyme	Compound	Homonym	Syllables	Phonemes
Habitats					
house	✓			1	3
home	✓			1	3
hut	✓			1	3
tent	✓			1	4
trailer				2	
treehouse		✓		2	
castle				2	4
mansion				2	
hogan				2	
igloo				2	4
apartment				3	
cellar				2	4
attic				2	4
porch				1	4
townhouse		✓		2	
cabin				2	
hotel				2	
cave	✓			1	3
tepee				2	4
flat	✓		✓	1	4
condominium				5	
houseboat		✓		2	
motel				2	
mobile home				3	
tower	✓			2	3
dungeon				2	
lighthouse		✓		2	
camper				2	
Home					
ceiling (sealing)			✓	2	
floor	✓			1	4
wall	✓			1	3
furniture				3	
couch				1	3
chair	✓			1	3
bed	✓			1	3
lamp	✓			1	4
table	✓			2	4
refrigerator				5	

VOCABULARY LIST

WORD	Rhyme	Compound	Homonym	Syllables	Phonemes	WORD	Rhyme	Compound	Homonym	Syllables	Phonemes
Home (continued)						**Other:**					
stove				1	4						
footstool		✓		2							
bookcase		✓		2							
fireplace		✓		2							
cupboard		✓		2							
doorbell		✓		2							
bathroom		✓		2							
bathtub		✓		2							
hallway		✓		2							
sink	✓		✓	1	4						
shower	✓			2	3						
School											
school	✓			1							
playground		✓		2							
sidewalk		✓		2							
flagpole		✓		2							
chalkboard		✓		2							
cafeteria				5							
gymnasium				4							
recess			✓	2							
teacher				2	4						
principal (principle)			✓	3							
office				2	4						
classroom		✓		2							
library				3							
desk				1	4						
book	✓			1	3						
math	✓			1	3						
reading				2							
write (right)	✓		✓	1	3						
swing	✓			1	4						
slide	✓		✓	1	4						
lunchtime		✓		2							
flag	✓			1	4						
pencil				2							
pen	✓		✓	1	3						
paper				2	4						
notebook		✓		2							
homework		✓		2							

UNIT 3
Sports—Hobbies

CONCEPTS

Unit 3 includes the players, rules and equipment of all kinds of sports. This theme is of immediate interest to nearly all students and their families.

VISUAL ENVIRONMENT

- Sports equipment cutouts (see pages 62 and 63)
- Winter Sports poster (Peabody Kit — Level K)
- Mounted pictures of sports (Obtain good pictures from *Sports Illustrated* and *Boys' Life* magazines.)
- Sports posters
- Store displays involving sports (Ask for them at your local grocery, drug or department stores.)
-
-
-
-
-
-
-
-

DISPLAYS

- **Sports Display:** Collect all kinds of sports equipment and uniform parts (ask the P.E. department and parents to help you). Items might include a baseball cap, swimming mask, hockey stick, badminton racquet and birdie, tennis racquet, golf ball and tee, croquet ball and mallet, skateboard, fishing pole, trophy, handball, etc. Label these.

- **Hobby Display:** Have the students bring in hobby items for a Hobby Show. Models, collections and crafts could be used for many language activities.

- **Ball Display:** Display all kinds of balls: marbles, ping pong ball, golf ball, tennis ball, baseball, softball, croquet ball, kickball, volleyball, basketball, football, sponge ball, inflatable ball, billiard ball, jack ball, bowling ball.

-

-

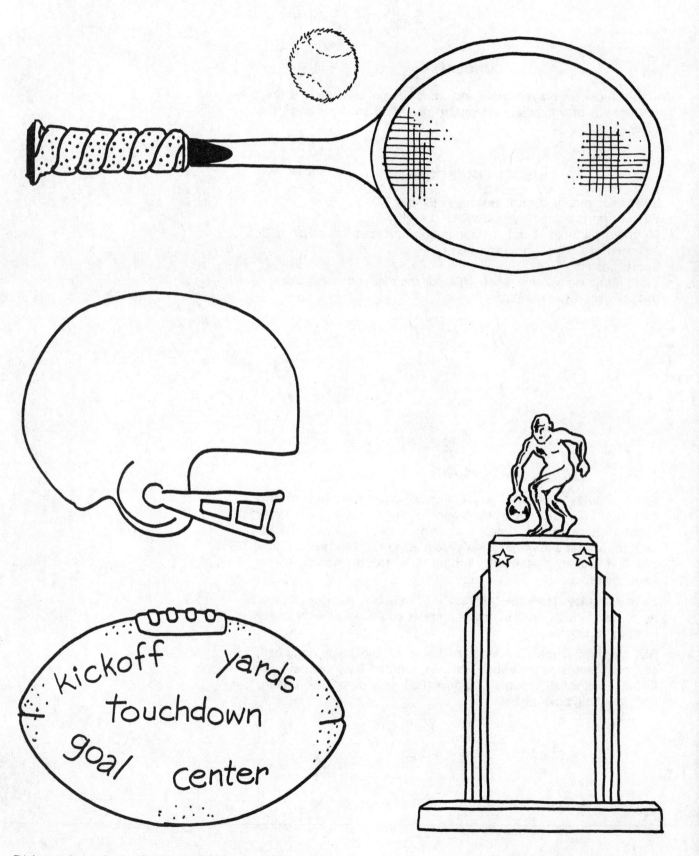

kickoff   yards
touchdown
goal   center

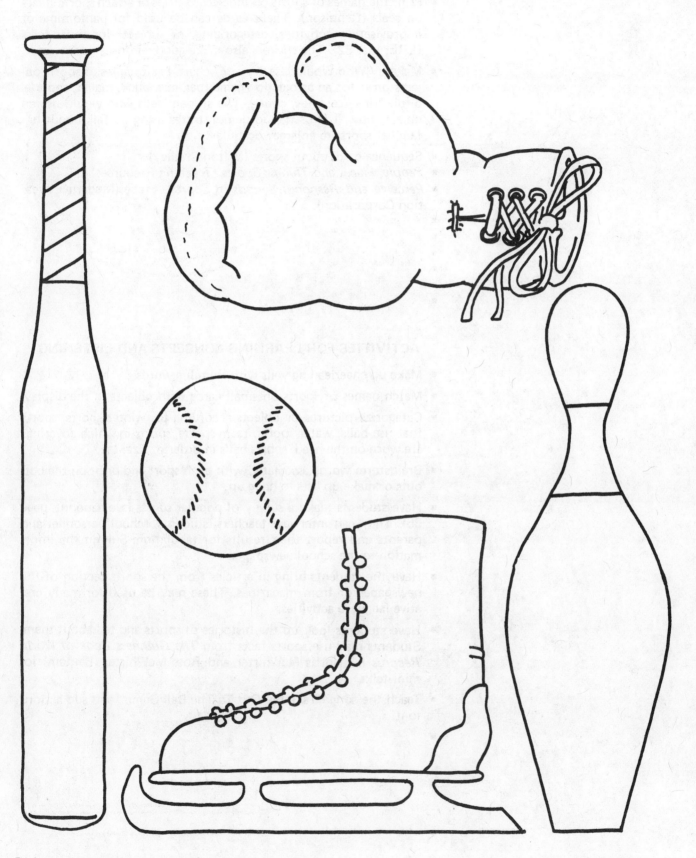

MATERIALS

- Print the names of sports on index card strips or attach sports stick-on seals (Dennison). These cards can be used for pantomime or improvisation activities, categorizing, or subjects for short talks (LRE, List 82). The stickers also make good reinforcers or rewards.

- Make a "Who Would Use A . . . ?" chart. Print names of sports objects on it for an association game (oar, cue, puck, mallet, snorkle, birdie, rink, tee, alley, court). The student tells who would use an object, how it is used, and demonstrates using it. Talk about unfamiliar sports to enlarge vocabulary.

- Sequence cards about sports (Milton Bradley)
- *People, Places and Things: Sports* (Teaching Resources)
- *Perceive and Respond: Sounds of Sports* — tape (Modern Education Corporation)
-
-
-
-
-
-

ACTIVITIES FOR LEARNING CONCEPTS AND LISTENING

- Make up cheerleading yells with rhyming words.
- Match names of sports on small cards with objects in the display.
- Categorize pictures or objects according to: winter sports, sports that use balls, water sports, team sports, sports in which coverings are worn on the head, sports balls in order of size, etc.
- Brainstorm words associated with each sport and print on the cutouts or make up lists to hang up.
- Have students make a survey of popular sports (see handout, page 66). They can interview teachers, students, school personnel and parents and report their results for tabulation. Submit the information to the school newspaper.
- Have the students bring in articles from the sports section of the newspaper or from magazines. These may be used for many creative language activities.
- Have students look up the histories of sports and tell about them. Students may use sports facts from *The Guinness Book of World Records* by Norris McWhirter and Ross McWhirter (Bantam) for mini-talks.
- Teach the song "Take Me Out To The Ball Game" and add actions to it.
-
-
-

HOME PROJECTS AND FIELD TRIPS

- Take a trip to a sports store or the sports section of a department store. Look at and talk about all the sports equipment. Tell your child all about one of the sports unfamiliar to him.

- Watch a sports program on television with your child. Notice the referee's signals and scoring systems. Explain the rules and unfamiliar terms to your child.

- See how many sports your family can list. The students can get all the help they want — from people, encyclopedias, books, etc. Return the list to school. (At school: You may wish to have a contest. A reproducible list form is included on page 66).

- Go to the library and find some books this week on sports and read them with your child.

- Play sports charades. Act out the sports on the vocabulary list.

- Try out a new sport. Make the equipment. Soda pop cans and a tennis ball make a good bowling set. A balloon and rolled-up newspapers can be used for badminton. Be creative! (At school: The students can tell about and demonstrate their new sports.)

- Invite the parents in for a hobby and sports day. Students can pantomime sports, put on a sports news-demonstration show, explain their hobbies, etc.

-

SKILLS LISTS

Phonology, Morphology, Syntax

- After the students return their sports lists, have them find the names that have long and short vowels:

long	*short*
bowling	swimming
diving	boxing
baseball, etc.	tennis, etc.

Rhyming Sentences (LRE, List 2)

The golf *ball* is very *small.*

The racing *car* went very *far.*

I left my *jacket* with my tennis *racquet.*

Look! There's an *icicle* on your *bicycle.*

I tripped over my *skis* and fell on my *knees.*

There are lots of *teachers* sitting in the *bleachers.*

What is the *name* of this silly *game?*

Look at his *face* as he runs in the *race!*

The boys made a *bet* that the ball would go through the *net.*

- For practice in rhyming, read *Stop That Ball* by Mike McClintock (Random House). Have the students fill in the rhyming words as you read.

_____   _____

_____   _____

_____   _____

_____   _____

_____   _____

_____   _____

_____   _____

_____   _____

_____   _____

Scrambled Sentences (LRE, Lists 15–16)

3 Words
swims fast Betty
high basketballs bounce
difficult is chess
three times jump
whistles referees use

4 Words
I further swim cannot
trout fisherman the catches
Jim plays well badminton
dangerous judo be can
the high jumps diver

Sentence Types

Basketball

That guard is very tall.	(declarative)
Can you pass the basketball?	(interrogative)
The coach is yelling so loud!	(exclamatory)
Don't foul out of the game.	(imperative)

- Other subjects for mini-books: *archery, hiking, umpires, awards.*

Question Game

Answers: into the target (**Question:** *Where* do you try to shoot an arrow?)

down the slopes
whistle
foul ball
through the hoop
the goalie
three strikes
"Safe!"
karate
in a stadium

- Have the student select a sports object or picture and ask a question about it. Another student answers the question.

"How do you play jacks?"
"What does a baseball player wear?"
"Where do you go ice skating?"

Irregular Verbs (LRE, List 11)

- There are many irregular verbs that apply to sports. You may wish to give your students some practice with these in the context of sports stories or in describing pictures or actions. For example:

  They are *beginning* the race.   He will *break* the record.
  They *began* the race.   He *broke* the record.

- Other verbs: *beat, catch, choose, dive, fall, fight, fly, hide, hurt, lose, ride, run, shoot, slide, spin, steal, strike, swim, swing, teach, throw, win, wind.*

Semantics

Homonyms (LRE, Lists 23–26)

- See vocabulary list.

- Make riddles:

  What word means *a kind of metal* and *to run to a base?"* (steel-steal)

  "What word means *a dance* and *the object you hit with a bat?"* (ball)

  "What word means *the grass around your house* and *36 inches?"* (yard)

Antonyms (LRE, Lists 28–30)

easy–hard	deep–shallow
high–low	beginning–end
fast–slow	strong–weak
win–lose	dangerous–safe
play–work	victory–defeat
crooked–straight	go–stop
forward–backward	foul–fair

Compound Words (LRE, Lists 21–22)

- See vocabulary list.

- There are many compound words associated with sports. List them and talk about why the two words were chosen to make up each compound word.

- Have the student write or tell a sports story or do an on-the-spot game description using compound words.

Adjectives and Adverbs (LRE, Lists 32–33)

- Show sports pictures to the students. Have them make up sentences about each picture using appropriate adverbs.

  The girl jumped rope *fast.*
  The football player kicked the ball *aggressively.*
  She ice skates very *gracefully.*

Basic Concepts and Following Directions
(LRE, Lists 19-20, 47-49)

- Set up a small obstacle course in the room or outdoors. Give the students directions to follow, starting with two and increasing the number as they progress:

    "Step over the board and hop to the tire."
    "Go through the hula hoop and drop the ball in the can."

Scrambled Sentence Sequence (LRE, Lists 41-42)

The batter swung at the ball. 2
The pitcher threw a curve. 1
The umpire called "Strike!" 3

I pasted it in my stamp book. 3
I cut the stamp off the envelope. 2
I received a letter with a pretty stamp. 1

He looked down the alley. 2
Jim picked up the bowling ball. 1
He rolled the ball toward the pins. 3

Andy served the volleyball over the net. 1
The ball flew over the wall and into the street. 3
Anne hit the ball hard. 2

Henry put on his backpack. 1
He slept in his sleeping bag. 3
He hiked a long way. 2

Incomplete Sentences (LRE, Lists 43–46)

We went sailing on the l_____.

The barbells were very h_____.

Surfers ride on the w_____ .

Cindy's ice skates were brand n_____.

John b_____ his leg while skiing.

Throw the basketball through the h_____.

I use a green mallet in c_____.

A touchdown is worth six p_____.

The u_____ wears a face mask.

- Let the students make up some!

Cognitive Tasks

Analogies (LRE, Lists 52–62)

Birdie is to *badminton* as *puck* is to _____ .	hockey
Golf ball is to *bumpy* as *croquet ball* is to _____ .	smooth
Court is to *tennis* as *track* is to _____ .	running
Slalom is to *skiing* as *backstroke* is to_____ .	swimming
Stake is to *horseshoes* as *target* is to_____ .	archery
Referee is to *football* as *umpire* is to_____ .	baseball
Stadium is to *football* as *rink* is to _____ .	ice skating
Surfboard is to *water* as *sled* is to_____ .	snow
Sail is to *sailboat* as *paddle* is to_____ .	canoe
Wet suit is to *scuba diving* as *gloves* are to _____ .	boxing

- Using the students' sports lists, make up more sports analogies with them. Talk about the relationship used in each analogy.

Classification (LRE, Lists 65–68)

- Present the items orally in mixed-up order. Which three go together best? Why?

putter, club, tee	dive
pole, snow, chairlift	fish
surfing, diving, swimming	bowling
batboy, homerun, pitch	kickoff
model, glue, instructions	score
trophy, award, medal	contest
helmet, facemask, goggles	football
tennis, golf, basketball	playground
golf ball, small, white	basketball
cheerleader, referee, player	game

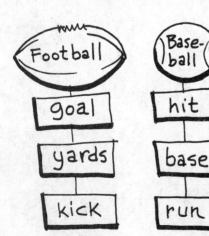

- Select words from three different sports categories on the vocabulary list. Print them on small cards. Have the students classify them under the proper headings.

Categories (LRE, Lists 63–64)

Sports in which you do not use a ball
Hobbies that involve collecting
Sports that involve an animal
Water sports
Things you wear for sports
Things you do in football
Places where you play different sports
Parts of a sailboat
Things in a gymnasium
Kinds of balls
Others:

- The balls from the display may be used for several activities:

ordering by size
giving descriptions
categorizing (common characteristics)
telling similarities and differences
telling how to play each game
making up riddles
Others:

Part-Whole Relationships (LRE, Lists 69–70)

An *inning* is part of a _____ (game) _____ .

A *player* is part of a _____ (team) _____ .

First base is part of the _____ (baseball diamond) _____ .

Diving board is part of a _____ (swimming pool) _____ .

Bleachers are part of a _____ (stadium) _____ .

Stirrups are part of a _____ (saddle) _____ .

Kickoff is part of a _____ (football game) _____ .

Wicket is part of a _____ (croquet set) _____ .

Cleats are part of a _____ (baseball shoe) _____ .

Sandtrap is part of a _____ (golf course) _____ .

- Make up easier ones for younger children.

Associations (LRE, Lists 71–73)

Baseball

base	grandstand	popcorn
bunt	infield	shortstop
cheering	inning	umpire
diamond	pennant	win
dugout	pitcher	

- Have the students tell a story "in the round." Each time you hold up a card with one of the above words on it, the next student must continue the story and use that word. When you hold up an "end" card, the student must end the story. Record and play back the story. Listen for story line, interesting vocabulary, fluency and good articulation.

- Other subjects for association: *swimming, bowling, camping.*

Similarities–Differences (LRE, Lists 74–76)

high jump-broad jump	jogging-racing
gallop-trot	sailboat-kayak
figure skating-hockey	sledding-skiing
bat-racquet	gymnasium-stadium
umpire-coach	inning-quarter

- Have two students act out the word pairs with dialogue. They are not allowed to use the two words, however.

Inferences (LRE, Lists 78–79)

I am used in a game. I have strings. I am used to hit a ball.	tennis racquet
I am a sport. I am played indoors. I am played on an ice rink.	hockey
I have numbers on me. People watch me during a game. My information keeps changing.	scoreboard
We are used in an indoor sport. There are twelve of us. A ball rolls and knocks us down.	bowling pins
People collect us. We come from many countries. We are used on letters.	stamps

Production of Language

Nonverbal (LRE, List 82)

- Act out sports individually or in small groups.
- Have students concentrate on specific actions.
- Also do the sports in slow motion. Call out names of other sports and have the students switch actions.
- Others:

Descriptions

- Each student picks a sports card and must tell how to play that sport, with the steps in proper sequence.
- Have each student give a "chalk talk" demonstrating some aspect of a sport. He may draw while he is talking or put his illustration on the chalkboard beforehand.
- Others:

Short Talks (LRE, List 97)

- Put on a sports news show and videotape it.
- Give a talk about your hobby. Bring in some items to show.
- Tell about a famous athlete's life.
- Interview Babe Ruth about his baseball career.
- Give a play-by-play description of a football, basketball or volleyball game starring some students in your class (make-believe).
- Give a television commercial for an electric tennis racquet.
- Be a coach and give a pep talk to your players before the big game.
- Introduce Mohammed Ali to the television audience.
- Others:

Improvisations (LRE, Lists 87, 96)

- You are on the lake in your boat. A big storm comes up. Your boat starts to fill with water. Show us what happens.
- You are playing basketball in a game. The referee blows the whistle and calls a foul. You disagree.
- You are in an archery tournament. Your first two arrows miss the target. Your last one hits the bulls eye!
- Your friend is up to bat in a baseball game. He strikes out and you lose the game. He feels terrible. What do you do?
- You and a friend are mountain climbing. You get lost. Show us what happens.
- You are fishing. Something pulls on your line. You reel it in and it is not a fish. What is it?
- You are bullfighting. Your bull turns out to be very tired or tame. Explain to the audience.

VOCABULARY LIST

WORD	Rhyme	Compound	Homonym	Syllables	Phonemes
Baseball					
baseball		✓		2	
softball		✓		2	
shortstop		✓		2	
infield		✓		3	
batboy		✓		2	
facemask		✓		2	
grandstand		✓		2	
backstop		✓		2	
plate	✓		✓	1	4
strike	✓		✓	1	4
fly	✓		✓	1	3
run	✓		✓	1	3
pitcher			✓	2	4
bunt	✓			1	4
slide	✓		✓	1	4
base	✓		✓	1	3
diamond			✓	2	
stadium				3	
dugout		✓		2	
Bowling					
bowling				2	
ball	✓		✓	1	3
alley			✓	2	3
pins	✓		✓	1	4
spare	✓		✓	1	4
line	✓		✓	1	3
strike	✓		✓	1	
Football					
football		✓		2	
kickoff		✓		2	
goalpost		✓		2	
touchdown		✓		2	
pigskin		✓		2	
lineman		✓		2	
signal			✓	2	
fumble				2	
tackle				2	4
pass	✓		✓	1	3
huddle				2	4

WORD	Rhyme	Compound	Homonym	Syllables	Phonemes
quarter			✓	2	
point			✓	1	4
referee				3	
yard	✓		✓	1	
official				3	
timeout		✓		2	
Basketball					
basketball		✓		3	
guard	✓			1	4
dribble				2	
net	✓		✓	1	3
shoot	✓		✓	1	3
coach			✓	1	3
defense				2	
practice				2	
hoop	✓			1	3
basket			✓	2	
foul (fowl)			✓	1	3
overtime		✓		3	
score	✓			1	4
cheerleader		✓		3	
trophy				2	
award				2	
prize	✓			1	4
medal				2	4
victory				3	
win	✓			1	3
lose	✓			1	3
tie	✓		✓	1	2
Hobbies					
hobby				2	4
collection				3	
craft				1	
model			✓	2	4
game	✓		✓	1	3
Other Sports					
handball		✓		2	
volleyball		✓		3	
tetherball		✓		3	

VOCABULARY LIST

WORD	Rhyme	Compound	Homonym	Syllables	Phonemes
Other Sports (continued)					
surfboard		✓		2	
shuffleboard		✓		3	
badminton				3	
horseshoes		✓		2	
judo				2	4
karate				3	
boxing				2	
wrestling				2	
sailing				2	
soccer				2	4
croquet				2	
polo				2	4
Archery					
archery				3	
arrow				2	
target				2	
bow	✓		✓	1	2
bullseye		✓		2	
Skiing					
ski	✓			1	3
downhill		✓		2	
chairlift		✓		2	
pole (poll)	✓		✓	1	3
snow	✓			1	3
skilift		✓		2	
Swimming					
pool	✓		✓	1	3
swimming				2	
backstroke		✓		2	
freestyle		✓		2	
dive	✓			1	3
crawl	✓		✓	1	4
relay				2	
race	✓		✓	1	3
team (teem)	✓		✓	1	3
board (bored)			✓	1	4

WORD	Rhyme	Compound	Homonym	Syllables	Phonemes
Golf					
golf				1	4
green	✓		✓	1	4
par	✓			1	3
club	✓		✓	1	4
sandtrap		✓		2	
putter	✓			2	4
tee (tea)	✓		✓	1	2
golfcart		✓		2	
Hockey					
hockey				2	
goalie				2	4
puck	✓			1	3
penalty				3	
rink	✓			1	4
stick	✓		✓	1	4
skate	✓			1	4
Tennis					
match	✓		✓	1	3
tennis				2	
court			✓	1	4
serve			✓	1	3
love			✓	1	3
backhand		✓		2	
set	✓		✓	1	3
grip	✓			1	4
racquet (racket)			✓	2	
player				2	
Other					

UNIT 4
Food—Farms—Stores—Money

CONCEPTS

Unit 4 investigates where our food and plants come from, how they are processed and used, and the working of farms. Stores and money are also covered.

VISUAL ENVIRONMENT

- Farm poster (Peabody Kit — Level K)
- Food cutouts (American Dairy Council; contact the local office)
- Farm mural (see pages 78–80)
- Pictures of food and displays obtained from local grocery stores
- Posters on foods, nutrition, food processing
-
-

DISPLAYS

- **Food Display:** Foods in several different forms, such as: potatoes (mashed, french fries, potato chips, potato bread, sweet potatoes, instant potatoes, baked, canned, etc.); corn (on the cob, corn flakes, corn oil, popped corn, canned, frozen, etc.); fruit in fresh, canned, frozen, jellied and dried forms.

- **Restaurant Display:** Menus, tray, dishes, placemats, order forms, aprons, cash register and play money, and a chef's hat. These can be used for discussions and dramatic play about restaurants and food.

Why not attach bits of straw or Easter grass and plastic fruits to your enlarged mural?

MATERIALS

- Plastic fruits and vegetables (Peabody Kit — Level K)
- Building Match-Ups (Developmental Learning Materials)
- Play Family farm set (barn and silo with animals; Fisher-Price)
- Food cards (GOAL — Milton Bradley)
- Coin collection (domestic and foreign)
- Before and After Puzzles (Trend)
- Farm Animal seals (Dennison)
- Paper plates
- Cooking utensils: spatula, sifter, strainer, nutcracker, cheese slicer, potato peeler, etc. (use these for categorizing, describing and learning functions)
- Real foods to taste
- Menus from different restaurants for creative language activities
- Seed packages and seeds from avocado, peach, cherry, etc.
- Farm and City Crossword Puzzles (Ideal)
-
-
-

ACTIVITIES FOR LEARNING CONCEPTS AND LISTENING

- Talk about foods, where they come from and how they grow. Compare and categorize, notice differences and similarities. Discuss size, color, shape, cooking and taste. Use the plastic fruits, seeds, Before and After puzzles and other materials.

- Discuss farms: animals, planting, equipment and harvest; use the farm mural.

- Have the students bring in food boxes, cans and labels. Look for weights, abbreviations, compound words, syllabication, beginning sounds, etc. Seed packages and menus also can be used.

- Have a taste test. Take one food, discuss how and where it grows and then sample it. Talk about the taste, smell and texture. Describe it (yellow, stringy, bitter, and so on). Think up recipes for it. Make a class book about the foods you tried.

- Show the students a coin collection with coins from different countries. They may also bring foreign currency from home. Compare and contrast; talk about values and decorations on the coins. Pinpoint on the map where the countries are from which the money originated.

- Talk about the foods in the food display. Discuss the different processes involved in changing the form of the food (for example, raw potato to potato chips, etc.).

- Visit the school cafeteria before lunch and see how the food is prepared, stored and disposed of.

- Collect several different kinds of pasta (macaroni, spaghetti, linguini, noodles, etc.). Have the students separate the mixture into types. Give descriptions of each kind.

- Play the "One Potato, Two Potato" game. Children stand in a circle and put out their fists. One person taps each fist in order while they say: "One potato, two potato, three potato, four; five potato, six potato, seven potato, MORE!" The child whose fist is tapped

Shopping

New Fruits
We found:

_____
_____
_____
_____

New Vegetables:

_____
_____
_____
_____

New meats:

_____
_____
_____

on "More" places his fist behind his back. The tapping continues with the chant until only one fist remains; that person wins. This is a good rhythmic language game for sequencing and memory.

- Have each child make up an advertisement for his favorite food. Encourage him to use descriptive adjectives and illustrations. Display the ads.

- Play and sing "The Farmer In The Dell" and "Old MacDonald Had A Farm."

- Set up a grocery store or restaurant for role-playing.

-

HOME PROJECTS AND FIELD TRIPS

- Encourage your child to help you with food preparation. Talk about recipes, kitchen utensils, appliances and foods.

- Play restaurant or store with your child. Take different roles each time you play — be a grandmother, a cowboy, a business manager, the waiter, a child, etc. Try to work in new vocabulary words as you play.

- Fill out the "New Foods We Found" list with your child when you and your child visit the grocery store. Return the list to school for sharing.

- Take a trip to a plant nursery. Talk about the different kinds of trees, flowers, bushes, leaves, etc. Help your child grow a plant at home.

- Give your child opportunities to use and count money. Take a trip to the bank and talk about what happens there. Encourage your child to ask questions: "How many safety deposit boxes are there?" "Where do you keep the money at night?" Let him open his own savings account. Explain what happens to the money.

- Help your child learn nursery rhymes involving foods: "Pease Porridge Hot," "Little Jack Horner," "Peter Piper," "Little Tommy Tucker," "The Queen of Hearts," and "Little Boy Blue." (Send home the words with the parent letter.)

-

-

SAMPLE LETTER

Dear Parents:

Our current language theme is <u>Foods-Farms-Stores-Money</u>. Please help your child expand vocabulary and concepts this week by doing these activities:

HOME PROJECTS AND FIELD TRIP

1. Take a trip to the <u>grocery store</u>.
    a. Look at the fruits and vegetables and talk about the ones that your child is not familiar with (artichoke, kale, limes, etc.). Talk about the size, shape, color, how you cook and eat them, and their similarity to other fruits and vegetables. Fill out the attached list with your child and let him bring it back to school to share.

    b. Look at the meats. Talk about which come from pigs, cows, sheep, etc. Talk about different kinds of fish we eat.

    c. Look at the dairy case. Discuss which products are made from milk and how they are made. Talk about kinds of cheese (difference in color, texture, smell, etc.).

2. In the <u>kitchen</u>: Let your child help with food preparation. Talk about what you are doing. Look through the utensils and name and discuss the use of each (spatula, sifter, tongs, pastry brush, etc.).

3. We will discuss <u>money</u>. If you have coins from other countries, perhaps let your child take one to school to tell about. Show him coins and let him sort and count them.

Your help is invaluable in the development of your child's language skills. Thanks for your cooperation.

Sincerely,

BOOKS AND PHONOGRAPH RECORDS

Books

- *Charlie Brown's Second Super Book of Questions and Answers: about the earth and space . . . from plants to planets!* (Random House).

- *Where Everyday Things Come From* (Platt and Munk).

- *Green Eggs and Ham* by Dr. Seuss (Random House).

- *Farms. Milk. Bread.* Wonder Books (Grosset and Dunlap).

- *The Farm Book* (Golden Press).

- *The Best Word Book Ever,* sections on foods, farms, kitchens (Golden Press).

- *The Fat Cat* (Scholastic Book Services).

- *Tall Tree — Small Tree* by Mabel Watts (Western Publishing Co.).

- *A Tree Is Nice* by Janice Udry (Harper and Row).

- *Mr. Rabbit and the Lovely Present* by Charlotte Zolotov (Harper and Row).

- *Strega Nona* by Thomas De Paola (Prentice Hall).

- *The Sweet Touch* by Lorna Balian (Abingdon Press).

- *Bread and Jam for Frances* by Russell Hoban (Harper and Row).

- *Three Stalks of Corn* by Leo Polite (Scribner).

- Traditional stories concerning foods and farms: *Peter Rabbit, Gingerbread Man, Little Red Hen, Stone Soup, Johnnie Appleseed.*

Records

- *Alphabet, Counting and Acting Out Songs,* "One Potato," "Farmer In the Dell" (Walt Disney).

SKILLS LISTS

Phonology, Morphology, Syntax

- For articulation practice, use carrier phrases, such as *"Sally likes to eat* soup, sandwiches, salad." Use food picture cards for target sound words.

- Have students categorize food picture cards according to beginning sounds. This may be done as a team game with the students taking turns. Place the cards under the appropriate letter labels.

- Do sound blending (LRE, Lists 7-10) practice with names of foods and with pictures in the farm mural. For example, "a—pp—le," "p—i—g," etc.

- Give each student a paper plate with four letters printed on it and a set of food pictures or cutouts. The students make up a dinner by finding one food that starts with each letter to put on the plate. For rhyming practice, print four words on the plate. The students must find foods that rhyme with the selected words.

- Others:

Rhyming Sentences (LRE, List 2)

Pigs' *feet* are a kind of *meat.*

Put a *sign* on the grape *vine.*

Dan went to the *beach* and ate a *peach.*

A honey *bee* flew up to the *tree.*

What is the *price* of a box of *rice?*

Today's the *day* we will bale the *hay.*

I bought a *lime* for just a *dime.*

I ate a *potato* and a big red *tomato.*

Bobby *fell* into the *well.*

Scrambled Sentences (LRE, Lists 15-16)

3 Words
spinach I like
serve waiters meals
eats Randy avocadoes
are sweet watermelons
cash checks banks

4 Words
billfold lose don't your
today harvested the farmer
a tractor dad drives
orange this rotten is
is vegetable a asparagus

Sentence Types

Scarecrow

A scarecrow frightens birds.	(declarative)
Does the scarecrow look real?	(interrogative)
Look at the crows fly!	(exclamatory)
Put a hat on the scarecrow.	(imperative)

- Other subjects for mini-books: *windmill, bank holdup, desserts.*

- Display the books in a prominent place in the school.

Question Game (See instructions in Unit I.)

Answers: a chef (**Question:** *Who* cooks the food in a restaurant?)
a pitchfork
in a restaurant
in the fall
brands the cattle
cash a check
the cashier
tomatoes
milk the cow
a pigpen
in the silo

- Ask other questions using *what, when and where.*

Semantics

Homonyms (LRE, lists 23-26)

- See vocabulary list.

Antonyms (LRE, Lists 28-30)

city-country	cold-hot
heavy-light	bitter-sweet
empty-full	sweet-sour
fat-skinny	warm-cool
work-play	moist-dry
sharp-dull	nourish-starve
gather-scatter	thaw-freeze
fertile-barren	tough-tender
sell-buy	cooked-raw
expensive-cheap	soft-hard
spend-save	fall-spring

- Have the students make up sentences about the farm, money or foods using these antonym pairs.

Compound Words (LRE, Lists 21-22)

- See vocabulary list.

Basic Concepts and Following Directions (LRE, Lists 47-49)

- Have each child give you directions for fixing his favorite food. Print the directions on a paper plate or on the apple story shape (page 92). Let him decorate the plate and put a pipe cleaner hanger on it to display at school and home. A sample from a student:

"First take out some spaghetti. Put some boiling water on the stove. Put the spaghetti in. Stir it and add the sauce. Pour out the water and put cheese on it. Then eat it!"

- The parents will certainly enjoy these. You may wish to read the recipes back to the students and talk about the sequence and specificity of the directions.

Idioms, Proverbs and Similes (LRE, Lists 36–40)

- What do they mean?

full of baloney	that's corny
finger in every pie	in a pickle
not my cup of tea	he's a ham
sour grapes	apple of your eye

Don't cry over spilt milk.
The proof of the pudding is in the eating.
A watched pot never boils.
Too many cooks spoil the broth.
An apple a day keeps the doctor away.
Money burns a hole in your pocket.

Scrambled Sentence Sequence (LRE, Lists 41–42)

He planted the corn.	2
The farmer plowed the field.	1
The corn grew six feet high.	3
The manager gave him his paycheck.	2
Sandy worked at the swimming pool.	1
He cashed his check at the bank.	3
The waitress took our order.	2
We went to the restaurant.	1
We ate delicious hamburgers.	3
The butcher cut up the cow.	1
John bought the meat.	3
She put the steaks in packages.	2
They made cheese and ice cream.	3
The cow gave some milk.	1
The farmer took it to the dairy.	2

- Have the students tell what happened next.

Incomplete Sentences (LRE, Lists 43–46)

Tomatoes grow on v _____ .

Coleslaw is made with c _____ .

Bill gave the w _____ a tip.

The horses are in the c _____ .

The farmer will p _____ the wheat.

The silo holds c _____ .

A sow is a female p _____ .

Oranges, limes and g _____ are citrus fruits.

Pickles are made from c _____ .

I like to eat c _____ for breakfast.

- If students are unfamiliar with some words, such as *silo*, give explanations to build vocabulary.

Cognitive Tasks

Analogies (LRE, Lists 52–62) Tell why.

Cucumber is to *pickle* as *grape* is to _____ .　raisin

Dollar is to *bill* as *nickel* is to _____ .　coin

Eggplant is to *vegetable* as *cantaloupe* is to ____ .　fruit

Cow is to *barn* as *horse* is to _____ .　corral

Bacon is to *pig* as *hamburger* is to _____ .　cow

Food is to *pancake* as *beverage* is to _____ .　milk/juice

Stalk is to *celery* as *pod* is to _____ .　peas

Orchard is to *trees* as *field* is to _____ .　crops/wheat

Well is to *low* as *windmill* is to_____ .　high

Classification (Lists 65–68)

wallet, vault, piggy bank	coin
cauliflower, lettuce, cabbage	orange
menu, waiter, cashier	dessert
pork, beef, poultry	potatoes
barn, silo, outhouse	tractor
coins, bills, change	wallet
apple, orange, peach	banana
trunk, roots, leaves	grow
cheese, ice cream, butter	eggs
milk, juice, tea	jelly

Categories (LRE, Lists 63–64)

Vegetables that grow underground
Parts of a tree
Kinds of meat
Animals on a farm
Kinds of desserts
Things a farmer does in his work
Kinds of stores
Things in a bank
Names for money
Beverages
Others:

Part–Whole Relationships (LRE, Lists 69–70)

A *blade* is part of a _____ (plow) _____ .

A *stem* is part of an _____ (apple) _____ .

A *dessert* is part of a _____ (meal) _____ .

Wool is part of a _____ (sheep) _____ .

A *quarter* is part of a _____ (dollar) _____ .

Steak is part of a _____ (cow) _____ .

Cob is part of an _____ (ear of corn) _____ .

A *vault* is part of a _____ (bank) _____ .

PART WHOLE

Core
Seed
Cob
Penny

- Make up a "Part-Chart." Print the parts. Students name the wholes and add other parts.
- Others:

Associations (LRE, Lists 71-73)

Bank

teller	vault	checks
bills	banker	robber
holdup	drive-through	loan
interest	guard	bank book
safety deposit box	computers	

- Other words for association: *butcher, scarecrow, cowboy.*
- Write one word on the chalkboard. Invite the students to add associated words during the week.

Similarities-Differences (LRE, Lists 74-76)

mushroom-toadstool	busboy-waiter
fruit-vegetable	stem-trunk
restaurant-cafeteria	appetizer-dessert
purse-wallet	horse-pony
sap-blood	peas-beans

Inferences (LRE, Lists 78-79)

I am a vegetable. I am green. I am used in salads.	lettuce
I am a tool. I am used on the farm. I look like a big fork.	pitchfork
I am round and metal. I have numbers on me. I am on a safe.	combination lock
I work in a restaurant. Very few people see me. I keep the dishes clean.	dishwasher
I am a kind of meat. I am ground up. I usually come from a pig.	sausage

Production of Language

Nonverbal (LRE, Lists 81-86)

- Pantomime eating foods. You may call out different foods and have students switch actions. "Corn on the cob — watermelon — ice cream cone — taffy — hamburger — cotton candy — pickle." Have the students concentrate on the taste, size and texture of the food and how they would handle it.
- Have the students act out nursery rhymes concerned with food. Discuss the poems first. Use "Jack Sprat," "Old Mother Hubbard," "Little Jack Horner," "Little Tommy Tucker," "Queen of Hearts," and "Little Boy Blue."

Descriptions (LRE, List 89)

- Use plastic foods. Play "I'm thinking of . . ." The student tries to give a complete description of one of the foods.

- Ask each student to think about and describe an *entire sequence* of processing a food. Examples:

  ice cream — from cow to carton
  carrot — from planting to eating
  hamburger — from cow to McDonald's
  peaches — from seeds to cans

Read the food sequences in *Where Everyday Things Come From* as an introduction (sugar, bread, chocolate, honey).

Storytelling

- These theme-related stories are good for storytelling projects or creative drama: *Peter Rabbit, Gingerbread Man, Little Red Hen, Stone Soup, Johnnie Appleseed.*

Short Talks (LRE, Lists 91–95)

- Tell how to cook your favorite food.
- Give a commercial for a food you bring in.
- Demonstrate how to make a banana split.
- Interview a farmer on what he does all day.
- Be a bank president and convince students they should save money.
- Tell how to saddle and ride a horse.
- Interview Jack Sprat and his wife.
- Give an on-the-spot report about Humpty Dumpty.
- Others:

Improvisations (LRE, Lists 87, 96)

- You are a waiter or waitress in an ice cream parlor. You bring a gooey banana split to a customer but accidentally spill it on him.
- You are a corn seed that has just been planted. Show us how you feel as the rain comes and you grow tall.
- You are a cowboy. You saddle your horse and go out riding but you get lost. What do you do?
- A robber comes into your bank and demands money. Show us what you would do.
- You get a telephone call. You have won $10,000. What do you do?
- Others:

Questions and Discussion Topics

- How can we tell how old a tree is?
- Why do leaves turn colors and fall off trees?
- What things do we use that come from plants (besides food)?
- How do bees make honey?
- What makes popcorn pop?
- Which plants are poisonous?

Suggest these in the home letter.

Story Shape

Story Shape

VOCABULARY LIST

WORD	Rhyme	Compound	Homonym	Syllables	Phonemes
Farming					
farm				1	4
horse				1	4
saddle				2	4
bridle (bridal)			✓	2	
reins (rains, reigns)			✓	1	4
tractor				2	
bale (bail)	✓		✓	1	3
silo				2	4
cowboy		✓		2	
barn				1	4
sow (sew, so)	✓		✓	1	2
plant			✓	1	
harvest				2	
windmill		✓		2	
pitchfork		✓		2	
haystack		✓		2	
scarecrow		✓		2	
outhouse		✓		2	
corral				2	
crops				1	
irrigate				3	
well	✓		✓	1	3
grain	✓		✓	1	4
Trees & Plants					
sap	✓		✓	1	3
tree	✓			1	3
seed	✓			1	3
vine	✓			1	3
bush				1	3
root	✓			1	3
trunk			✓	1	
bark	✓		✓	1	4
pod	✓			1	3
stem	✓		✓	1	4
limb	✓			1	3
plant			✓	1	
branch				1	
leaf				1	3
stalk			✓	1	

WORD	Rhyme	Compound	Homonym	Syllables	Phonemes
Meat & Cooking					
cattle				2	
beef				1	3
pork				1	4
poultry				2	
veal	✓			1	3
meat (meet)	✓		✓	1	3
butcher				2	
hot dog		✓		2	
bake	✓			1	3
broil	✓			1	4
boil	✓		✓	1	3
fry	✓			1	3
mix	✓			1	3
diet				2	
calories				3	
Foods & Restaurant					
restaurant				3	
tablecloth		✓		3	
busboy				2	
waiter				2	4
dishwasher		✓		3	
chef				1	3
menu				2	4
dessert				2	
appetizer				4	
beverage				3	
Fruits & Vegetables					
fruit	✓			1	4
vegetable				3	
asparagus				4	
eggplant		✓		2	
beet (beat)	✓		✓	1	3
beans				1	4
lettuce				2	
tomato				3	
watermelon		✓		4	
orange			✓	1	
grape	✓			1	4
lemon				2	

VOCABULARY LIST

WORD	Rhyme	Compound	Homonym	Syllables	Phonemes
Fruits (continued)					
apple				2	3
peach				1	3
grapefruit		✓		2	
banana				3	
Money					
money				2	4
bill	✓		✓	1	3
cash (cache)	✓		✓	1	3
coin				1	3
change			✓	1	4
check	✓		✓	1	3
billfold		✓		2	
wallet				2	
tip	✓		✓	1	3
bank	✓		✓	1	4
safe			✓	1	3
paycheck		✓		2	
bankbook		✓		2	
deposit				3	
receipt				2	
price	✓			1	4
combination				4	
vault			✓	3	
Other:					

WORD	Rhyme	Compound	Homonym	Syllables	Phonemes
Other (continued)					

UNIT 5
Animals

CONCEPTS

Unit 5 considers land animals, their natural habitats, their use and behavior. This subject appeals to students of all ages.

VISUAL ENVIRONMENT

- Animal pictures (from the American Dairy Council; contact your local office)
- Animal posters (every month *Instructor* and *World* magazines include beautiful and interesting posters; *World* also has good animal pictures for mounting on construction paper, and excellent animal articles)
-
-
-
-

DISPLAYS

- **Animal Display:** Collect all kinds of stuffed animals and toy plastic animals. These may be categorized into jungle, farm, circus, forest, desert, wild, tame animals, etc. Make labels for the categories. (Ask the PTA to collect these for you. The children can also bring in their favorites to add to the display.)

-

-

MATERIALS

- Animal jigsaw puzzles (GOAL — Milton Bradley)
- Fairy Tale Finger Puppets (Milton Bradley)
- Animal picture cards (Peabody Kit — Level 2)
- Animal stickers (Dennison or Eureka)
- See-quees Stories — *Three Bears, Three Billy Goats,* and other animal stories (Judy)
- *Perceive and Respond: Animal and Insect Sounds* — tape (Modern Education Corporation)
- Classification/Logical Order Picture Cards — animals (Milton Bradley)
- Mix n' Match Puzzles — Animals and Their Young (Trend)
-
-
-

ACTIVITIES FOR LEARNING CONCEPTS AND LISTENING

- There are many excellent animal books and records (see Books and Phonograph Records). Read and discuss them with the students. You may wish to concentrate on one category of animals at a time, such as jungle or forest animals, and center all activities around that category.

- Teach nursery rhymes about animals: "Three Blind Mice," "Baa, Baa, Black Sheep," "Little Bo Peep," "Hey Diddle, Diddle," "Tom, Tom, the Piper's Son," "Pussy Cat, Pussy Cat." Send the words home for home practice.

- Discuss animal homes, coverings, habits, food and facts. Compare, contrast, categorize, list new information on charts.

- Talk about animal footprints and tracks.

- Teach words and actions to "There Was An Old Lady Who Swallowed a Fly."

-

-

-

HOME PROJECTS AND FIELD TRIPS

- Take a trip to the zoo and talk about all the animals with your child. Which animals have spots or stripes? What do they eat? What kind of feet or coverings do they have? Which animals are dangerous?

- Go to the library and check out some books on animals. Read them with your child.

- Play animal hospital or pet store with your child. Use toy or stuffed animals. Take turns being veterinarian, pet shop owner, customer. Introduce new vocabulary words as you play. "Do I need a *hutch* for the rabbit to live in?" "My lion's *mane* is falling out."

- Play "20 Questions" in the car or at the dinner table. One person thinks of an animal and the others ask questions (a limit of 20) to find out what it is. "Does it have horns?" "Does it live in the jungle?"

- Act out different animals and guess what they are (a good party game). You can also call out animal names, saying "Be a lion (cow, giraffe, donkey, etc.)." The children all imitate the animal until the next one is called out.

-

-

-

BOOKS AND PHONOGRAPH RECORDS

Books

- *Animals Do the Strangest Things* by Leonore and Arthur Hornblow (Random House).

- *Charlie Brown's Super Book of Questions and Answers: about all kinds of animals . . . from snails to people!* (Random House).

- *Wild and Woolly Animal Book* by Nila Jonas (Random House).

- *Hide and Defend* by Kathleen Daly (Golden Books).

- *Animal Homemakers* by Aurelius Battaglia (Platt and Munk).

- *Put Me In The Zoo* by Robert Lopshire (Random House).

- *Best Word Book Ever,* animals in categories (Golden Press).

- *The Cat In The Hat Comes Back* by Dr. Seuss (Random House).

- Traditional stories about animals: *Aesop's Fables, Three Billy Goats Gruff, Three Bears, Three Pigs, Brer Rabbit, Bambi, Ferdinand the Bull, Just So Stories.*

Records

- *The Sesame Street Book and Record* (Columbia).

- *Peter and The Wolf* (MGM).

- *Just So Stories* (Disneyland).

- *Mother Goose Nursery Rhymes* (Disneyland).

SKILLS LISTS

Phonology, Morphology, Syntax

- Use carrier phrases to practice articulation or grammatical forms. Turn over an animal card or go through animal picture books for the visual stimulus.

  "I saw a _____ in the forest."
  "The kangaroo *has* _____." "The bear *has* _____."
  "What is he doing?" "He is running."

- For practice in beginning sounds, have students make up sentences about animals:

  Annie Anteater ate apples.
  Bernie Bug bought berries.
  Cathy Cat cooked cake.

Rhyming Sentences (LRE, Lists 1–2)

The little *mouse* went into the *house.*

The big black *bear* sat in the *chair.*

We found a *skunk* in a pile of *junk.*

My puppy *chews* on my dad's old *shoes.*

We bought a *bunny* with our *money.*

The billy *goat* ate my new *coat.*

The baby *pig* is not very *big.*

The fat old *sheep* went to *sleep.*

Our dog will *bark* when it gets *dark.*

- Read *Cat In The Hat Comes Back* or *Put Me In The Zoo* and let the students fill in the rhyming words.

Scrambled Sentences (LRE, Lists 15–16)

3 Words
mean are bears
dogs bones chew
elephants trunks have
tigers for watch
me scare mice
stink skunks little

4 Words
my monkey is this
bears the feed don't
KingKong a gorilla is
eats the shark fish
in holes live rattlesnakes

Sentence Types

Farm Animals

The herd of cattle grazes here.	(declarative)
Did you feed the hogs yet?	(interrogative)
The ewe had three lambs!	(exclamatory)
Give the mare some oats.	(imperative)

- Other subjects for mini-books: *monkeys, dinosaurs, the zoo.*

Question Game

Answers: black and white   (**Question:** *What* color is a zebra?)
in the desert
Bugs Bunny
in a stable
penguins
with his trunk
eats bananas
quills
a buffalo
King of the Jungle

- To practice question forms, each student may ask a question about one animal in the display and another student answers. You may wish to select the question word to be used.

    "What do rabbits eat?" *"Where* do elephants live?"

Semantics

Homonyms (LRE, Lists 23-26)

- See vocabulary list
- Others:

Antonyms (LRE, Lists 28-30)

wild–tame	old–young
asleep–awake	fat–skinny
noisy–quiet	hungry–full
graceful–clumsy	healthy–sick
attack–defend	little–big
dangerous–safe	male–female
swift–slow	strong–weak

Adjectives and Adverbs (LRE, Lists 31-33)

- Each student selects an animal in the visual environment. He must write or say a sentence using at least four adjectives and/or adverbs.

    The *huge, hairy, brown* gorilla jumped *angrily.*
    The *tall, skinny, spotted* giraffe ate *anxiously.*

- Put up a list of adjectives and adverbs to choose from.

-

"Noisy as a _____ !"

Basic Concepts and Following Directions (LRE, Lists 19, 20, 47-49)

- Show a picture of an animal to one child. He gives directions to the other students so that they can draw it.

    "First draw a fat round body. Then draw a small head with a big mouth. Put four big teeth in the mouth. Add four fat short legs."

- Show the drawings when he is finished to check giving and following directions.

Idioms, Proverbs and Similes (LRE, Lists 36-40)

monkey business	cry wolf
dark horse	dog-eared pages
don't horse around	underdog
wolf in sheep's clothing	wild-goose chase
black sheep	go ape

Curiosity killed the cat.
A barking dog never bites.
You can't teach an old dog new tricks.
Don't change horses in the middle of the stream.
When the cat's away, the mice will play.

- Talk about why these animals were chosen for *similes* (LRE, List 35).

quiet as a mouse	stubborn as a mule
sly as a fox	hairy as an ape
cross as a bear	gentle as a lamb

- Think up new ones, such as:

noisy as a _____	_____ as a cow
fuzzy as a _____	_____ as a buffalo
graceful as a _____	_____ as a raccoon
shaggy as a _____	_____ as a goat
friendly as a _____	_____ as a tiger

Scambled Sentence Sequence (LRE, Lists 41-42)

They went over a fence.	3
The horse started to run.	2
Maria got on her horse.	1
A monkey did tricks.	2
We went to the zoo.	1
We laughed.	3
Kim drank the milk.	3
The cow gave milk.	1
The farmer delivered the milk.	2
Stephanie chased her mouse.	3
Stephanie opened the mouse cage.	1
The mouse ran out.	2
He fell down.	3
He tried to run.	2
Bambi was born in the forest.	1

Incomplete Sentences (LRE, Lists 41–42)

King Kong is a huge g_____ .

The monkey was swinging through the t_____.

Bambi was a f_____ .

Lions live in the j_____.

The hungry donkeys ate the h_____.

Did you hear the h_____ neigh?

The rabbit's h_____ is very clean.

The bear c_____ up the tree.

We leave our dog in a k_____ when we're gone.

The l_____ has a furry mane.

Cognitive Tasks

Analogies (LRE, Lists 52–62)

Apple is to *red* as *hippopotamus* is to _____ .   grey

Dog is to *tame* as *lion* is to _____ .   wild

Cow is to *horns* as *deer* is to _____ .   antlers

Fox is to *den* as *monkey* is to _____ .   tree

Horse is to *whinney* as *kitten* is to _____ .   meow

Man is to *doctor* as *animal* is to _____ .   veterinarian

Duck is to *quack* as *lion* is to _____ .   roar

Dog is to *paws* as *horse* is to _____ .   hooves

Pig is to *skin* as *sheep* is to _____ .   wool

Sow is to *piglet* as *doe* is to _____ .   fawn

Classification (LRE, Lists 65–68)

gorilla, orangutang, chimpanzee   rabbit
dog, coyote, wolf   beaver
doe, buck, bunny   cub
cow, barn, hay   squirrel
elephant, monkey, tiger   cow
oink, purr, neigh   horse
flock, herd, pack   cave
stable, kennel, burrow   hibernate
squirrel, chipmunk, skunk   elephant
squeal, snout, pig   claws

Categories (LRE, Lists 63–64)

Farm animals
Animals that we eat
Animals that eat meat
Furry animals
Noises animals make
Kinds of animal homes
Tame animals
Others:

▪ Make a chart with names of mother, father and baby animals (see page 105).

> sheep — ewe, ram, lamb
> pig — sow, boar, piglet

You may wish to send home the unfinished list for the family to work on with their child.

Part-Whole Relationships (LRE, Lists 69-70)

A *paw* is part of a ___(dog)___ .

Spots are part of a ___(leopard)___ .

A *hoof* is part of a ___(horse)___ .

Horns are part of a ___(bull)___ .

Cages are part of a ___(zoo)___ .

A *pouch* is part of a ___(kangaroo)___ .

Quills are part of a ___(porcupine)___ .

Vines are part of a ___(jungle)___ .

A *snout* is part of a ___(pig)___ .

A *corral* is part of a ___(ranch)___ .

Associations (LRE, Lists 71-73)

▪ Use any animal. Make mobiles.

HORSES
ride	saddle	bridle
hay	cowboys	western movies
gallop	rent	flies
corral	lasso	

POLAR BEARS
cold	white	fur
fish	huge	Antarctica
teeth	hunt	

Similarities-Differences (LRE, Lists 74-76)

lion-tiger	forest-jungle
hippopotamus-elephant	stable-corral
moose-deer	tiger-cat
horse-donkey	tusk-antler
bunny-teddy bear	lioness-cub

Inferences (LRE, Lists 78-79)

I live on a farm.   cow
I am big and I eat hay.
I give milk.

I am black and white.   skunk
I live in the forest.
Sometimes I give off a bad smell.

I am a very fat animal.   hippopotamus
I like to stay in the water.
Birds pick at my teeth.

I live in the forest.	beaver
I gnaw on trees.	
I build dams.	

I was a very large animal.	dinosaur
I had a long neck.	
I am now extinct.	

- Have the students make up their own clue sets for other animals.

Groups of Animals

army of ants
swarm of bees
bloat of hippopotami
pride of lions
tower of giraffes
gaggle of geese
den of snakes
troop of kangaroos
knot of toads
sloth of bear
colony of beavers

crash of rhinos
leap of leopards
litter of puppies
flock of sheep/chickens/geese
pack of wolves
nest of rabbits
business of flies
school of fish
herd of buffalo/deer/elephants/
    whales

Animal Family Names

Animal	Mother	Father	Baby
horse	mare	stallion	colt/foal/filly
cow	cow	bull	calf
chicken	hen	rooster	chick
deer	doe	buck	fawn
pig	sow	boar	piglet
goat	nanny	billy	kid
rabbit	doe	buck	bunny/kit
duck	duck	drake	duckling
bear	sow	boar	cub
turkey	hen	gobbler	chick
cat	puss/tabby	tom	kitten
dog	dam	sire	puppy
buffalo	cow	bull	calf
sheep	ewe	ram	lamb
lion	lioness	lion	cub
elk	cow	bull	calf
goose	goose	gander	gosling
kangaroo	doe	buck	joey
whale	cow	bull	calf
seal	cow	bull	pup

Production of Language

Nonverbal (LRE, Lists 81–86)

- Pantomime animals (see Home Projects, page 97).

-

Descriptions

- Put on a "Pet Parade" show. Tape record it or use a video tape recorder if possible. Have each child bring in an animal (stuffed, toy or picture) and tell all about it. Put up a cue card with the following clue words:

    name, what it looks like, what it eats, where it lives, what it does (runs very fast, builds dams), and the noise it makes.

Storytelling (LRE, List 90)

- Have each child dictate a story to you about an animal adventure. Print the story on the animal story shape. Read it back to the students, using lots of expression.

    Some samples:

    "Once I had a horse. It was black. He fell in a hole. I pulled him out. He was stuck. So I sold him."   by Lucy (grade 1)

    "I had four puppies. One was named Snoopy. One was named Snowflake. The third puppy was Daisy and the fourth was Ricky. Ricky bit Snoopy in the ear. Snoopy squealed. He ran to his mother. Their mom brought them back to the doghouse."
    by Tony (grade 2)

- Send home the stories to be read and displayed.

Short Talks (LRE, Lists 91–95)

- Suggested topics:
    The Animal I Would Most Like To Be
    How To Give Your Dog a Bath or Teach Him Tricks
    How To Saddle and Ride a Horse

- Give a commercial for a restaurant just for cats.

- Give a commercial for treats that make your pet fly.

- Pretend you are an animal, and tell what you do all day (where you sleep, how you get food, what you do for fun, and so on).

Improvisations (LRE, Lists 97, 96)

- You are walking your dog in the park when he sees a cat and becomes very excited. What will happen?

- You are a veterinarian. Someone brings in an animal you have never seen before. Show us what happens.

- You are animals in the forest. You hear a deer hunter coming. You are afraid and want to protect the young animals. Decide what to do.

- You are Tarzan of the Jungle. You find a chimpanzee that you can train.

- You are cavemen. You go out hunting. You see dinosaurs.

- Act out some *Aesop's Fables* or *Just So Stories*. Then make up new ones about animals.

Questions and Discussion Topics

- Why do dogs pant?

- Why do cats' eyes shine at night?

- How can bears hibernate and not eat every day?

- What do elephants use trunks for?

"Do like Tarzan...

... swing on vine!"

Story Shape

VOCABULARY LIST

WORD	Rhyme	Compound	Homonym	Syllables	Phonemes
Animals					
animal				3	
cow	✓			1	2
pig	✓			1	3
dog	✓			1	3
cat	✓			1	3
goat	✓			1	3
sheep	✓			1	3
rabbit				2	
mouse	✓			1	3
groundhog		✓		2	
deer (dear)	✓		✓	1	3
squirrel				2	
skunk	✓			1	
bear (bare)	✓		✓	1	3
buffalo				3	
wolf				1	4
lion				2	4
tiger				2	4
elephant				3	
giraffe				2	
zebra				2	
rhinoceros				4	
hippopotamus				5	
gorilla				3	
leopard				2	
monkey				2	
ape	✓			1	2
kangaroo				3	
dinosaur				3	
anteater		✓		3	
Animal Sounds					
bark	✓		✓	1	4
trumpet			✓	2	
squeak	✓			1	
neigh (nay)	✓		✓	1	2
squeal	✓			1	
oink				1	3
moo	✓			1	2
growl	✓			1	4
roar	✓			1	3
howl				1	3

WORD	Rhyme	Compound	Homonym	Syllables	Phonemes
bray	✓			1	3
meow				2	
Habitats					
cave	✓			1	3
den	✓		✓	1	3
forest				2	
pen	✓		✓	1	3
kennel				2	
ranch				1	4
doghouse		✓		2	
stable			✓	2	
hole (whole)	✓		✓	1	3
hutch				1	3
sty	✓			1	3
burrow				2	
zoo	✓			1	2
jungle				2	
desert				2	
Parts of Animals					
tusk				1	4
antlers				2	
quill	✓		✓	1	4
hoof				1	3
tail (tale)	✓		✓	1	3
snout	✓			1	4
claw	✓			1	3
paw	✓		✓	1	2
horn	✓		✓	1	4
pouch				1	3
mane (main)	✓		✓	1	3
whiskers				2	
Other					
veterinarian				6	
hibernate				3	
nocturnal				3	
extinct				2	
wild				1	4
tame	✓			1	3
mammal				2	
prehistoric				4	
instinct				2	

UNIT 6
Bodies of Water—Fish—Birds

CONCEPTS

Unit 6 surveys bodies of water and the creatures that live in them, insect life, and feathered creatures.

VISUAL ENVIRONMENT

- Ocean mural (see pages 110–112). Add old jewelry to the treasure chest, and netting, seashells and other ocean items to the mural.
- Posters of fish, birds and insects. See *World* and *Instructor* magazines for interesting posters and good pictures for mounting.
-
-

DISPLAYS

- **Ocean Display:** seashells, starfish, coral, acquarium or fishbowl with fish. Students may bring items from home to add to the display.
- **Birds and Insects Display:** different kinds of eggs, feathers, a nest, a bird in a cage, insect collections, plastic replicas of feathered creatures.
-
-

ACTIVITIES FOR LEARNING CONCEPTS AND LISTENING

- Print students' names on small paper fish to attach to the ocean mural. Talk about the mural, about going down in the ocean and what you might see: different kinds of fish, plants, a treasure chest, an old ship, sharks, whales. Imagine going down in a bathysphere. What would you wear? How long could you stay down? Use the mural for activities on the skills lists.
- Read the Wonder Starter books listed on the Books and Phonograph Records page: *Birds, Eggs, Bees, Whales, The Sea.* These introduce diverse ideas and vocabulary associated with each subject.
- Brainstorm all the different kinds of birds, insects, reptiles and fish. Make lists to use in other activities.

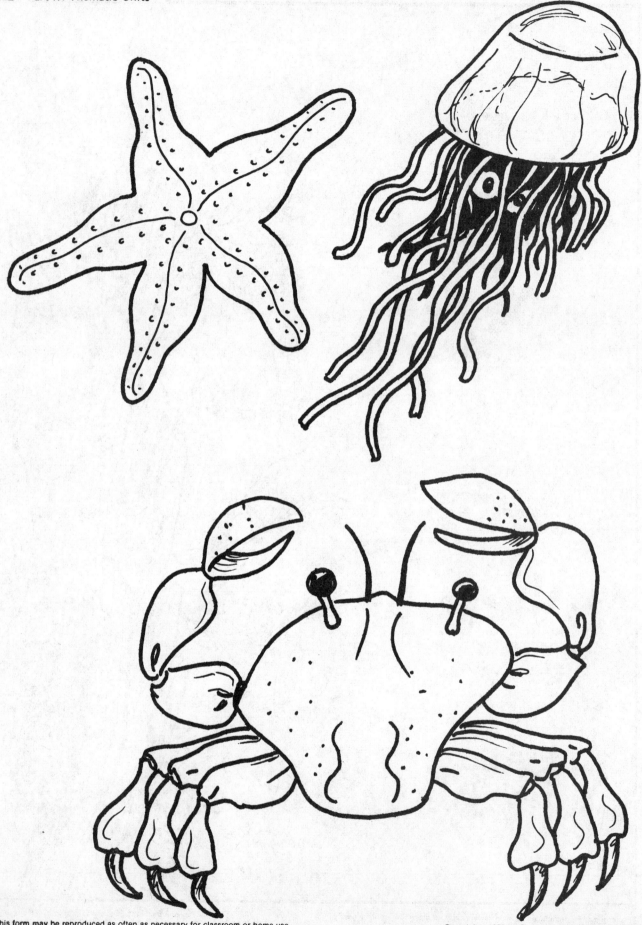

- Look at slides of oceans, fish and birds if you have them. They may be available through your library, or a parent might be willing to bring some in to show.

- Teach the students "Eentsy-Weentsy Spider" fingerplay and poems such as "Hickity Pickety," "Sing a Song of Sixpence," "Humpty Dumpty," "Ladybird, Ladybird, Fly Away Home," and "I Know An Old Lady Who Swallowed a Fly."

- Talk about insects and birds and their habits. Look at items in the display; make up riddles, classify, categorize, describe, etc.

-

-

HOME PROJECTS AND FIELD TRIPS

- Take a trip to the pet store. Observe and talk about the fish in the acquarium, the birds and crustaceans. Discuss their colors, how they move, their shapes and what they eat.

- Take a trip to a park where there are ducks, fish and boats. Talk about fishing and equipment. Go fishing if you can.

- Encourage your child to bring seashells to school if you have some so he can share information about them.

- When you are outdoors, listen for birds singing. Look for insects and talk about what they do, which ones sting, what they eat, and so on.

- Make a milk carton bird feeder (see parent letter).

SAMPLE LETTER

Dear Parents:

Our language theme for the next two weeks will be <u>Bodies of Water-Fish-Birds</u>. Please help your child expand his or her vocabulary and concepts by doing these activities:

HOME PROJECTS AND FIELD TRIPS

1. Take a field trip to a <u>pet store</u> and look at the birds and fish. Talk about the differences in color, shape, size and body parts. Discuss what they eat and how they swim or fly.

2. Make a milk-carton <u>bird feeder</u> (see illustration) to hang outside your home. Put seeds or bread crumbs in it and watch for visits from birds.

3. <u>Look at books</u> about fish, birds and oceans. If your child does not have a library card from the Public Library, this would be a good time to get one and start the library visiting habit.

4. If you have <u>seashells</u> at home, look at and talk about them with your child. Let him take some to school to show to his group.

VOCABULARY AND DISCUSSION STARTERS

octopus, seahorse, lobster, oyster, tuna, seaweed, island, tide, lighthouse, oceanographer, pelican, ostrich, stork, peacock, swan, hawk, extinct, beach, seagull, pirate, ships

1. What makes the tide come in and go out?

2. What is down at the bottom of the ocean?

3. How do fish breathe in the water?

If you are not sure of the answers, look them up with your child. Thank you for your help.

Sincerely,

BOOKS AND PHONOGRAPH RECORDS

Books

- *The Hungry Caterpillar* (Scholastic Books).

- *Reptiles Do The Strangest Things, Birds Do The Strangest Things,* and *Fish Do The Strangest Things* by Leonora and Arthur Hornblow (Random House).

- *Eggs. Birds. Whales. Bees. Butterflies. The Sea.* Wonder Books (Grosset and Dunlap).

- *The Bird Book* (Golden Press).

- *Charlie Brown's Super Book of Questions and Answers: about all kinds of animals . . . from snails to people!* (Random House).

- *Best Word Book Ever,* sections on birds and fish (Golden Press).

- Traditional stories: *Chicken Little, Little Red Hen, The Tortoise and the Hare.*

Records

- *Burl Ives' Animal Folk* record; songs about fish and fowl (Disneyland).

A little bee
stung my knee!

SKILLS LISTS

Phonology, Morphology, Syntax

- For sound blending practice, say the names of birds and marine animals and objects on the ocean mural: "s–t–or–k," "sh–ar–k." The student names the animal or bird and makes up a sentence about it (LRE, Lists 7-10).

- Rhyme (LRE, Lists 1–2) words with objects on the mural. For example:

   SHARK: ark, bark, dark, mark, park
   NET: bet, wet, pet, met, set
   CHEST: west, vest, nest, rest, dressed

   Then help the students make up mini-poems.

   The *shark* swam in the *park* in the *dark.*
   The bird wore a *vest* on his *chest* in his *nest.*

- Use the vocabulary list in making up exercises for individual skills.

Rhyming Sentences

   Look at the *seal* eat his *meal.*
   Put the slimy *fish* on the little *dish.*
   I saw a spider *crawl* right up the *wall.*
   A little *bee* stung me on the *knee.*
   I started to *shiver* when I swam in the *river.*
   The little green *frog* chased the black *dog.*
   Can a *hawk* learn to *talk?*
   Put the *feather* in the hat made of *leather.*
   The black *bat* flew over my *hat.*
   The yellow *duck* waddled under the *truck.*

Scrambled Sentences (LRE, Lists 15-16)

   3 Words
   pinches crab the
   the flooded river
   spouts have whales
   buzzing bees are
   owls that hoot

   4 Words
   treasure buried the pirates
   let's sand castles build
   slow the turtles crawl
   spider bit me a
   is beautiful butterfly the

Sentence Types (Make mini-books.)

   Crocodile
   That crocodile has bumpy skin.   (declarative)
   Do you know how long he is?   (interrogatory)
   Look at his teeth!   (exclamatory)
   Stay away from swamps.   (imperative)

- Other subjects: *sea monster, scuba diving, mermaids, goldfish.*

Question Game (See instructions in Unit I.)

    Answers: eight arms   (**Question:** *What* does an octopus
                                              have to grab things with?)

                in a treasure chest
                gills
                penguin
                migrate
                spins a web
                quack
                in a cage
                a bat
                seashells

Semantics

Homonyms (LRE, Lists 23–26)

- There are many homonym pairs in this unit. Talk about them and have the students illustrate the two meanings (tied-tide). Display these in a prominent place in the school. Make a class homonym book with illustrations.

Antonyms (LRE, Lists 28–30)

below–above	dangerous–safe
over–under	liquid–solid
wet–dry	swift–slow
sink–float	in–out
lower–raise	deep–shallow
high–low	attack–defend
ugly–pretty	heavy–light
empty–full	old–new

- Using an antonym pair, a student may describe something in the ocean mural.

    "The octopus is *ugly* but the seahorse is *pretty.*"

Compound Words (LRE, Lists 21–22)

- See vocabulary list.
- Match the word parts written on separate cards.

Basic Concepts and Following Directions (LRE, Lists 19–20, 47–49)

- Use the visual environment ocean mural. Give each child directions to follow, such as:

    "Put your fish *behind* the shark."
    "Make your fish swim *over* the eel."
    "Put your fish *next to* the treasure chest."

Idioms, Proverbs and Similes (LRE, Lists 36–40)

- Talk about the meanings; then have the students act out the idioms and others guess which ones they are doing.

crocodile tears	as the crow flies
card shark	fish out of water
sounds fishy	wild goose chase
eats like a bird	kill two birds with one stone
stool pigeon	stir up a hornet's nest

Birds of a feather flock together.
The early bird catches the worm.
A bird in the hand is worth two in the bush.

- Look at the ocean mural and have the students think of *similes* using the following adjectives:

slimy as ___an octopus___   deep as _____

slippery as ___an eel___   vicious as _____

wiggly as _____   colorful as _____

fast as _____   fragile as _____

heavy as _____   swift as _____

green as _____   slow as _____

scary as _____

- Make up a chart with the adjectives and nouns in two columns in random order. The students match the appropriate pairs.

Scrambled Sentence Sequence (LRE, Lists 41-142)

A beautiful butterfly came out.	3
The caterpillar crawled on the tree.	1
He made a chrysalis.	2
A big wave came up on the beach.	2
We built a sand castle.	1
It washed away our castle.	3
The whale blew water out of his spout.	1
The whalers saw him.	2
They shot a harpoon.	3
The eggs hatched.	2
Mother duck laid some eggs.	1
Some little ducklings crawled out.	3
He caught a fly.	3
The spider waited.	2
The spider spun a web.	1

Incomplete Sentences (LRE, Lists 43–46)

The octopus waved his wiggly a_____.

The sea diver wore a pair of f_____ .

The shark has sharp t_____ .

Did the mosquito b_____ you?

The scarecrow scared the b_____ .

We found a s_____ on the beach.

The bat h_____ upside down.

Will you have t_____on Thanksgiving?

The robin made a n_____ in the tree.

- Have the students make up a second related sentence for each one. For example:

The octopus waved his wiggly *arms.*
The sea diver saw him and s_____ to safety.

Cognitive Tasks

Analogies (LRE, Lists 52–62)

Crab is to *pincers* as *octopus* is to _____ . tentacles

Trout is to *stream* as *dolphin* is to _____ . ocean

Caterpillar is to *stripes* as *ladybug* is to _____ . spots

Duck is to *quack* as *owl* is to _____ . hoot

Whale is to *harpoon* as *fish* is to _____ . hook

River is to *bank* as *ocean* is to _____ . shore

Robin is to *fly* as *catfish* is to _____ . swim

Puddle is to *safe* as *swamp* is to _____ . dangerous

Crocodile is to *reptile* as *beetle* is to _____ . insect

Bird is to *feathers* as *fish* is to _____ . scales

Classification (LRE, Lists 65–68)

ocean, lake, pond	beach
fly, dive, glide	peck
feather, scales, pincers	fish
screech, hoot, squawk	bark
aquarium, nest, cage	eagle
line, pole, reel	fishing
gills, fin, tail	shark
canal, river, stream	lake
moth, butterfly, wasp	spider
turtle, snail, crab	seal

Categories (LRE, Lists 63–64)

Kinds of birds that can't fly

Kinds of insects

Bodies of water

Noises birds make

Things you find on the beach

Things that have shells

Things a fisherman uses

- Categorize shells in the display: rough and pointed, round and smooth, smooth and shiny, etc.

Part-Whole Relationships (LRE, Lists 69–70)

- These may have several answers. Remind the students that the answer will be related to the theme.

A *tusk* is part of a ___(walrus)___ .

A *spout* is part of a ___(whale)___ .

Sand is part of the ___(beach)___ .

A *pearl* is part of an ___(oyster)___ .

A *fin* is part of a ___(fish)___ .

Tentacles are part of an ___(octopus)___ .

A *stinger* is part of a ___(bee)___ .

A *shell* is part of a ___(snail)___ .

A *wing* is part of a ___(bird)___ .

Associations (LRE, Lists 71–73)

Whale

spout	huge	killer
Moby Dick	ocean	mammal
Sea World	smooth	shiny

Pirate

eye patch	gangplank	mutiny
boots	bandana	beard
deck	peg–leg	cannon
ship	ale	sword

- Other subjects: *cocoon, oceanographer, vulture.*   /ULTURE

- Make up stories!

Similarities–Differences (LRE, Lists 74–76)

porpoise–whale	sting–bite
parrot–canary	jellyfish–octopus
duck–swan	frog–toad
stream–river	cockroach–spider
butterfly–moth	aquarium–fishbowl

- Draw a card with a set of words on it. Tell two similarities and two differences about the set. The other students guess the two words. For instance:

  porpoise–whale   "They both live in the ocean."
  "They both have spouts."

  "One is much larger than the other."
  "One can leap out of the water."

Inferences (LRE, Lists 78–79)

I live in the sea.   shark
I swim very fast.
I have sharp teeth and big jaws.

I am very cold   iceberg
I stick up out of the ocean.
I am made of ice.

I am green.   alligator
I am dangerous.
I live in a swamp.

I live in the trees.   woodpecker
I make a lot of noise.
I peck holes in trees.

I sleep all day.   bat
I catch insects at night.
I sleep hanging upside down.

Production of Language

Nonverbal (LRE, Lists 81–86)

- Print the words listed below on small cards. Students draw cards and act out the words. Remind them to use facial expressions as well as body movement to convey their messages. Do frequent demonstrations for them.

mermaid	lighthouse	seal
lobster	pelican	penguin
eel	shark	crocodile
squid	quicksand	pirate
submarine	sand castle	butterfly
spider	inchworm	turkey
cuckoo	eagle	fisherman
kayak	whale	

Storytelling (LRE, List 90)

- After you have discussed the mural and sealife, have the students dictate stories about sea adventures. Print the stories on the whale story shapes. The students may color the whales on the other side. Put up a display in a prominent place in the school. The students may also make flannel board stories and tell them to another group.

Some samples:

THE GOLDEN FISH
I was going down to the bottom of the ocean. I was looking around and I saw a golden fish coming. It was swimming after me. It almost got my leg. I swam real fast and I saw somebody else in the water. It was Jimmy. I swam over to him and told him about the golden fish. We got out of ther fast!

Anita (grade 2)

THE TREASURE CHEST
Once upon a time I went down in the ocean. An electric eel came so I hid as fast as I could. Rocks started falling and I fell into a cave. I saw a really old ship so I went in it. I found two little fish and a whole bunch of diamonds and pearls. I swam up to the ship and I was rich.

Jimmy (grade 1)

Short Talks (LRE, Lists 91–95)

- Interview a deep sea diver who has discovered an underwater city.

- Tell how to build a birdhouse.

- Demonstrate how to draw a fish.

- Tell the story of Captain Nemo.

- Tell about a day in the life of a bee.

- Give a sales talk for a seahorse as a pet.

- Tell why we should make sea (salt) water into fresh.

- Tell all about the islands of Hawaii; do it as a travelogue.

Improvisations (LRE, Lists 87, 96)

- You are a deep sea diver. You find a treasure chest. Suddenly you see a shark. Somehow you get away safely.

- You are a spider. You spin a web and wait to catch an insect.

- You are a seal who does tricks. Show what you are thinking as your trainer works with you.

- You are fishing from a boat. You catch something. Show what happens.

- Act out the story of "The Tortoise and the Hare."

- Act out an ocean voyage with several students.

Questions and Discussion Topics

- How does an oyster make pearls?

- How do snakes and snails walk?

- How do bees make honey?

- Why do lightning bugs light up?

- How do spiders spin webs?

- See *Charlie Brown's Super Book of Questions and Answers* for more good questions. Suggest some of these in the parent letter for home discussions.

Story Shape

VOCABULARY LIST

WORD	Rhyme	Compound	Homonym	Syllables	Phonemes
Bodies of Water					
ocean				2	4
sea (see)	✓		✓	1	2
lake	✓			1	3
river				2	4
pond				1	4
stream	✓			1	
puddle				2	4
swamp				1	
island				2	
quicksand		✓		2	
tide (tied)	✓		✓	1	3
wave	✓		✓	1	3
shore	✓			1	3
sand	✓		✓	1	4
beach (beech)	✓		✓	1	3
iceberg		✓		2	
dam	✓			1	3
canal				2	
wharf				1	4
underwater		✓		4	
bank	✓		✓	1	4
Water Creatures					
crab	✓		✓	1	4
lobster				2	
octopus				3	
seahorse		✓		2	
oyster				2	
tuna				2	4
swordfish		✓		2	
catfish		✓		2	
shark	✓			1	4
goldfish		✓		2	
seaweed		✓		2	
seashell		✓		2	
starfish		✓		2	
seagull		✓		2	
seal	✓		✓	1	3
whale	✓			1	3
turtle				2	4
frog	✓			1	4

WORD	Rhyme	Compound	Homonym	Syllables	Phonemes
porpoise				2	
alligator				4	
crocodile				3	
fish	✓			1	3
walrus				2	
snail	✓			1	4
penguin				2	
jellyfish		✓		3	
snake	✓			1	4
reptile				2	
eel	✓			1	2
Other					
aquarium				4	
pirate				2	
treasure				2	
fishnet		✓		2	
Insects and Birds					
mosquito				3	
butterfly		✓		3	
yellowjacket		✓		4	
inchworm		✓		2	
ladybug		✓		3	
moth				1	3
bee (be)	✓		✓	1	2
caterpillar				4	
insect				2	
spider				2	
beetle				2	4
roadrunner		✓		3	
woodpecker		✓		3	
hummingbird		✓		3	
mockingbird		✓		3	
bluebird		✓		2	
lovebird		✓		2	
hawk	✓		✓	1	3
quail	✓			1	4
stork	✓			1	
parrot				2	
owl	✓			1	2
eagle				2	3
duck	✓		✓	1	3

VOCABULARY LIST

WORD	Rhyme	Compound	Homonym	Syllables	Phonemes
swallow			✓	2	
dove				1	3
canary				3	
robin				2	
chicken				2	
crow	✓		✓	1	3
turkey				2	4
fowl (foul)			✓	1	3
nest	✓			1	4
feather	✓			2	4
egg	✓			1	2
wing	✓			1	3
beak	✓			1	3
bill	✓		✓	1	3
Movements					
perch			✓	1	3
fly	✓		✓	1	3
soar (sore)	✓		✓	1	3
peck	✓		✓	1	3
screech	✓			1	
quack			✓	1	4
migrate				2	
sting	✓			1	4
crawl	✓			1	4
bite	✓			1	3
swim	✓			1	4
dive	✓			1	3
glide	✓			1	4

WORD	Rhyme	Compound	Homonym	Syllables	Phonemes
Other					

UNIT 7
Weather—Seasons—Time—Measurement

CONCEPTS

Unit 7 covers types of weather, precipitation, seasonal changes, time concepts, and measurement of volume, distance, weight, temperature, speed, and time.

VISUAL ENVIRONMENT

- Winter mural (see pages 128–130)
- Winter sports poster (Peabody Kit — Level K)
- Seasons posters (GOAL — Milton Bradley)
- Word cards (time, measurement, and weather words on index card strips)
-
-
-

DISPLAYS

- **Time Display:** all kinds of clocks (alarm, stopwatch, digital, electric, wristwatch, sand timer, cuckoo, sundial). They need not be working. Also display a calendar, metronome, etc.

- **Measuring Display:** tape, yardstick, ruler, scale, measuring cups, spoons, thermometer, barometer, speedometer, and other measuring instruments. Label the categories and group objects under labels (volume, speed, distance, temperature, weight).

-

MATERIALS

- All kinds of sequence cards (Developmental Learning Materials, Milton Bradley, Learning Development Aids, etc.)
- See-quees story puzzles (Judy)
- Globe and flashlight for demonstration of day and night
- *Perceive and Respond: Sounds of Weather* — tape (Modern Education Corporation)
- Mix n' Match Puzzles: Before and After, Sequence Level I (Trend)
-
-
-
-

Attach tufts of cotton for snow and a cotton tail on the rabbit. Add real feathers to the bird and make three-dimensional snowflakes.

ACTIVITIES FOR LEARNING CONCEPTS AND LISTENING

- Talk about the seasons and the changes that take place. Discuss what we do in different seasons, what we wear, how we feel.

- Discuss the weather with the winter mural as the takeoff point. What kinds of precipitation are there? Make word cards as the students think of weather words and add the cards to the mural.

- Use a scale to weigh things in the room. Demonstrate a metronome and use a stopwatch. Talk about the other objects in the display. Use the thermometer indoors and outdoors to see the changes.

- Cut apart old calendars. Have the students put months in order. Play games with days, months and numbers.

- Teach the students songs and poems, such as: "It's Raining, It's Pouring," "Hickory Dickory Dock," "Wee Willie Winkie," "30 Days Hath September." Show them how to remember the number of days in a month by counting on their knuckles.

- Do an evaporation experiment with a small amount of water in a dish.

- Make clocks out of paper plates and play time games. Let the students take them home to use.

- Demonstrate with a globe and flashlight how we have day and night on the earth.

- Talk about different kinds of storms. Discuss clouds. Go outdoors and observe signs of seasons and cloud formations.

- Read *Charlie Brown's Second Book of Questions and Answers* for other interesting concepts.

- Use the small object set for comparisons of size (see Appendix A).

HOME PROJECTS AND FIELD TRIPS

- Get a calendar for your child and mark important dates and holidays with him. Help him mark off days as they pass. Practice saying the days and months in order.

- Watch the television weather report with your child. Talk about the satellite cloud maps and the different kinds of weather.

- Go outdoors and watch a sunrise or sunset together. Also observe the clouds and see if you can see "pictures" in them.

- Use a ruler and measure lots of things in your house.

- Make a "Family Feet" poster (see parent letter).

- Play "remember when?" games. Ask your child if he remembers a certain event in his life (vacation, birthday party, special movie, etc.). Have him tell you everything he remembers about it. Praise him for recalling details.

- Play with water or sand and use measuring spoons, cups, funnels, pitchers, etc. Talk about the measurements as you play.

- Find all the measuring instruments around your house and make a list of them. Have your child take the list to school.

SAMPLE LETTER

Dear Parents:

Our new theme is <u>Weather-Seasons-Time-Measurement</u>. During the next two weeks please help your child expand vocabulary and concepts by doing these activities:

HOME PROJECTS

1. Find and talk about <u>things</u> <u>that</u> <u>measure</u> around your house:
   temperature: thermometer, oven controls
   time: clocks, timers, watches, calendar, etc.
   weight: scales (also at the store and Post Office)
   distance: yardstick, tape measure, odometer
   volume: measuring cups and spoons, milk cartons
   and food cans (gas pump at the service
   station)
   Make a list of all the measuring instruments and give
   it to your child to take to school.

2. Make a "<u>Family</u> <u>Feet</u>" <u>poster</u>. Your child can draw around a foot of each person (and pet) in the family. Measure each one to see the size relationships. Send the poster to school to share.

3. Watch a <u>weather</u> <u>report</u> on television with your child. Talk about forecasts, differences in temperatures, what humidity is, etc.

VOCABULARY AND DISCUSSION TOPICS

sunrise, sunset, rainbow, flood, weathervane, hail, fog, dew, cyclone, frost, blizzard, cloudburst, evaporate, whirlwind, forecast, months of the year, seasons of the year

Thank you for your help.

Sincerely,

BOOKS AND PHONOGRAPH RECORDS

Books

- *Rain. Night. Snow. Clocks.* Wonder Books (Grosset and Dunlap).

- *Charlie Brown's Second Book of Questions and Answers: about the earth and space . . . from plants to planets!* (Random House).

- *Greatest Word Book Ever,* sections on weather and seasons (Golden Press).

- *Winnie the Pooh and the Blustery Day* (Golden Press).

- *Short and Tall* by Richard Scarry (Golden Press).

- *Big Bird and Little Bird's Big and Little Book* (Golden Press).

- *Fast/Slow — High/Low* by Peter Spier (Doubleday).

- *The January Fog Will Freeze a Hog* by Ed Hubert Davis (Crown Publishers).

- Traditional stories: *Cinderella, Sleeping Beauty, Bambi, Rip Van Winkle, The Hare and The Tortoise.*

NOTES

SKILLS LISTS

Phonology, Morphology, Syntax

- This unit is good for working on tense. Use sequence cards for past, present and future tenses and for irregular verbs. Relate tense to time concepts that you have already discussed.

- Display labels of *Yesterday, Today* and *Tomorrow.* A student selects an action picture, describes the action, and places the picture under the correct label.

He *is crying.*	Today
They *built* a house.	Yesterday
The mouse *will eat* the cheese.	Tomorrow

Rhyming Sentences (LRE, Lists 1-2)

Is there a *lock* on the grandfather *clock?*
We weighed the *pail* on the *scale.*
Do you have *time* to spend a *dime?*
There's not much *light* during the *night.*
We saw a *fawn* in the woods at *dawn.*
Jasper took a *train* in the pouring *rain.*
The puppy will *freeze* in that cold *breeze.*
I take a *shower* every *hour.*
The plumber came last *week* to fix the *leak.*
Patti couldn't see her *dog* because of the *fog.*

Scrambled Sentences (LRE, Lists 15-16)

3 Words
snow melts the
freezing you are
broke the clock
thunder me scares
alarm the rang

4 Words
coach a stopwatch uses
a snowman made we
pounds eighty weigh I
the is weather rainy
what time it is

Sentence Types

Earthquake

An earthquake can do a lot of damage.	(declarative)
Have you ever felt an earthquake?	(interrogative)
Help! The earth is shaking!	(exclamatory)
Get under a table.	(imperative)

- Other subjects for mini-books: *rainbow, blizzard, snowballs.*

Question Game

Answers: stand on a scale   (**Question:** *How* do you weigh yourself?)

midnight
an hourglass   (**Question:** *What* has sand in it and tells time?)

kinds of moisture
during a storm
use a stopwatch
36 inches   (**Question:** *How many* inches are in a yard?)

weather forecaster   (**Question:** *Who* tells us if it will rain the next day?)

a cuckoo clock
sunrise
an umbrella
inside a building   (**Question:** *Where* should you go when a bad storm starts?)

Semantics

Homonyms (LRE, Lists 23–26)

- See vocabulary list. Print **homonyms** on small cards. Give two students a card and they must act out the two meanings of the word (rain–rein).

Antonyms (LRE, Lists 28–30)

old–new/young
heavy–light
modern–ancient
future–past
night–morning
summer–winter
spring–fall
day–night

midnight–noon
clear–hazy
freeze–melt
sunrise–sunset
cold–hot
cool–warm
fast–slow

Compound Words (LRE, Lists 21–22)

- There are many compound words associated with this theme. Discuss the two words which make up each compound word. Hang up a list of the words. Have the students tell a story "in the round" using as many of the compound words and lists as they can.

  One morning at *daybreak* I put on my *snowshoes* and went *outside.* I looked at the *windsock.* "There must be a *duststorm* coming," I said. I saw a *whirlwind.*

Adjectives and Adverbs (LRE, List 31)

- Brainstorm kinds of storms and associated words (blizzard, thunder, cyclone, etc.). Print the words on cards. Each student draws a card and gives an on-the-spot description using appropriate adjectives.

  "There is a *blinding* blizzard outside. The *cold* wind is blowing the ice off the *frozen* trees."

Past... Future...

Scrambled Sentence Sequence (LRE, Lists 41–42)

Pete put on his snowsuit and went outside.	2
It began to snow.	1
He built a snowman.	3
The pilot took off in his plane.	1
The pilot landed the plane quickly.	3
A storm started.	2
They saw and heard an avalanche.	2
Don and Jill went skiing.	1
They hurried to the ski lodge.	3
We put a dish of water outside.	1
The water evaporated.	2
The next day it was all gone.	3
Susie had eggs for breakfast.	1
She had steak for dinner at six p.m.	3
She had a sandwich at noon.	2

Incomplete Sentences (LRE, Lists 43–46)

The clock strikes t _____ at midnight.

There was white f _____ on the grass this morning.

W _____ is my favorite season.

The tourists visited an a _____ city.

The h _____ did a lot of damage along the beach.

The weathervane shows which way the w _____ is blowing.

Debbie was afraid of the l _____ during the storm.

The c _____ move fast across the sky.

How much did you w _____ on that scale?

During the snowstorm we wore our b _____ .

- Make up sentences that would logically follow each of the above sentences.

Cognitive Tasks

Analogies (LRE, Lists 52–62)

Ounce is to *pound* as *minute* is to _____ .	hour
Speedometer is to *speed* as *thermometer* is to __ .	temperature
Spring is to *summer* as *fall* is to _____ .	winter
Blizzard is to *snow* as *cloudburst* is to _____ .	rain
See is to *lightning* as *hear* is to _____ .	thunder
Cold is to *freeze* as *hot* is to _____ .	melt
Hours are to *clock* as *days* are to _____ .	calendar
Cold is to *winter* as *hot* is to _____ .	summer
Halloween is to *October* as *Christmas* is to _____ .	December
Monday is to *weekday* as *Saturday* is to _____ .	weekend

- Help students make up sequence analogies, such as:

    A is to *F* as *B* is to __.
    Saturday is to *Sunday* as *Thursday* is to _____.

Classification (LRE, Lists 65–68)

rain, snow, hail	cloud
hour, century, day	time
hazy, overcast, windy	forecast
calculator, ruler, stopwatch	inches
avalanche, earthquake, flood	thunder
December, May, June	Wednesday
pint, ounce, gallon	foot
sunrise, midnight, noon	hour
freezing, cold, cool	warm

- Name more words that go with the first three and tell how they go together:

    rain, snow, hail, *frost, dew, sleet* (types of precipitation)

Categories (LRE, Lists 63–64)

Kinds of clocks
Kinds of precipitation
Measurement words
Kinds of storms
Things you measure with
Things you wear when it is cold
Things you do when it is hot

Part-Whole Relationships (LRE, Lists 69–70)

A *minute* is part of an _____(hour)_____ .

A *pendulum* is part of a _____(clock)_____ .

Mercury is part of a _____(thermometer)_____ .

A *forecast* is part of a _____(weather report)_____ .

Thunder is part of a _____(storm)_____ .

A *month* is part of a _____(year)_____ .

An *ounce* is part of a _____(pound)_____ .

Colors are part of a _____(rainbow)_____ .

Water is part of a _____(cloud)_____ .

A *dial* is part of a _____(speedometer)_____ .

Associations (LRE, Lists 71–73)

Thunderstorm

lightning	rain	scared
wind	flood	crackling
summer	flash	wading
dark	loud	rainbow

Other subjects: *future, sunrise, rainbow, winter.*

- When the students are naming words, join in to model diversified ideas for them.

Similarities–Differences (LRE, Lists 74–76)

pound–quart	clock–watch
spring–summer	weathervane–compass
sunrise–sunset	weather report–forecast
rain–hail	scale–yardstick
cyclone–whirlwind	earthquake–avalanche

Inferences (LRE, Lists 78–79)

I am a beautiful sight. I am made of light. You see me after a rainstorm.	rainbow
I am a summer month. There is a celebration on one of my days. People shoot firecrackers.	July
I am very soft. I am cold and white. You can build a snowman with me.	snow
I help you keep track of time. I have lots of numbers. I am made of paper.	calendar
I talk a lot. I use maps and gadgets. I give the forecast.	weather forecaster

Logical Sequences (LRE, List 80)

- Make word cards for the following sequences. Have the students put them in proper order.

    second–minute–hour–day–week–month–year–decade–century
    morning–noon–afternoon–evening–night–midnight
    ounce–pint–quart–½ gallon–gallon

- Also do days of the week, months, seasons.

Production of Language

Production of Sentences (LRE, List 88)

- Give the student a three-word group from the list below with or without a visual cue. The student makes up a sentence using the words in any order. He or another student then can make up a second sentence that would logically follow the first. For example:

boat–wind–blew   The *wind blew* the *boat* across the lake.
                              The boat capsized and sank.

    snowstorm–winter–cold
    hands–clock–six
    cyclone–damage–house
    bright–lightning–storm
    football–fall–game
    icicle–melt–sun
    sunrise–beautiful–ocean
    fog–accident–highway
    cloud–sky–moves
    stopwatch–race–coach

Storytelling

- Some good stories that involve time are *Cinderella, Sleeping Beauty, Rip Van Winkle* and *The Hare and The Tortoise.*

- Make up stories about:

    One Stormy/Rainy Day . . .

    Print them on the cloud story shapes. Send the shape home and ask parents to print the story as the child dictates. Return it to school.

Short Talks (LRE, Lists 91–95)

- Give a television or radio weather report. Use visual aids such as a map or pictures of storms, clouds, etc.

- Make up or recite a poem about weather.

- Give an on-the-spot report of a cyclone passing through town.

- Describe in detail one of the timepieces in the display.

- Demonstrate how an hourglass or sundial works.

- Tell about the worst storm you have been in.

- Invent a new kind of clock and give a commercial for it.

Improvisations (LRE, Lists 87, 96)

- You are an alarm clock. Show and tell us how it feels to be set and to ring your alarm.

- A person from the future meets a person from ancient times. Discuss and show how you travel, what you eat, what you wear.

- You are Jack Frost and are bringing winter. Show and tell us what weather and moisture you brought.

- Act out Noah and the great flood.

- Act out the story of Rip Van Winkle.

- Do the story of Sleeping Beauty.

Questions and Discussion Topics

- What makes a rainbow?

- What makes a cloud?

- What is smog?

- How do weather forecasters know what the weather will be like?

- What is cloud seeding?

Story Shape

VOCABULARY LIST

WORD	Rhyme	Compound	Homonym	Syllables	Phonemes
Time					
spring	✓		✓	1	
summer				2	4
winter				2	
fall	✓		✓	1	3
autumn				2	4
season			✓	2	
year	✓			1	3
month				1	4
week (weak)	✓		✓	1	3
day	✓			1	2
night (knight)	✓		✓	1	3
calendar				3	
sunrise		✓		2	
sunset		✓		2	
midnight		✓		2	
noon	✓			1	3
hour (our)	✓		✓	1	2
minute				2	
second		✓		2	
century				3	
dawn (don)	✓		✓	1	3
dusk				1	4
daybreak		✓		2	
nightfall		✓		2	
weekend		✓		2	
future				2	
past (passed)	✓		✓	1	4
modern				2	
ancient				2	
Weather					
ice	✓			1	2
rain (rein, reign)	✓		✓	1	3
snow	✓			1	3
fog	✓			1	3
dew (do, due)	✓		✓	1	2
sleet	✓			1	4
hail	✓		✓	1	3
frost	✓			1	
cloud				1	4
moisture				2	

WORD	Rhyme	Compound	Homonym	Syllables	Phonemes
smog	✓			1	4
humidity				4	
precipitation				5	
freeze	✓			1	4
thaw	✓			1	2
melt	✓			1	4
icicle				3	
rainbow		✓		2	
snowdrift		✓		2	
cloudburst		✓		2	
rainstorm		✓		2	
thunderstorm		✓		3	
whirlwind		✓		2	
duststorm		✓		2	
lightning				2	
blizzard				2	
cyclone				2	
hurricane				3	
tornado				3	
avalanche				3	
monsoon				2	
earthquake		✓		2	
windsock		✓		2	
weather	✓			2	
snowball		✓		2	
snowflake		✓		2	
cold	✓		✓	1	4
hot	✓			1	3
temperature				4	
forecast		✓		2	
Measurement					
thermometer				4	
weathervane		✓		3	
hourglass		✓		2	
sundial		✓		3	
stopwatch		✓		2	
clock	✓			1	4
pendulum				3	
watch			✓	1	3
metronome				3	
measure				2	4

VOCABULARY LIST

WORD	Rhyme	Compound	Homonym	Syllables	Phonemes
Measurement (cont.)					
time	✓			1	3
yardstick		✓		2	
ruler			✓	2	4
weight (wait)	✓		✓	1	3
height	✓			1	3
degree			✓	2	
inch				1	3
yard	✓		✓	1	4
foot			✓	1	3
meter	✓		✓	2	4
liter	✓			2	4
pound	✓		✓	1	4
ounce				1	3
mile	✓			1	3
quart	✓			1	
pint				1	4
gallon				2	
scale	✓		✓	1	4
speedometer				4	
calculator				4	

WORD	Rhyme	Compound	Homonym	Syllables	Phonemes
Other:					

UNIT 8
Occupations

CONCEPTS

Unit 8 attempts to expand the students' knowledge and vocabulary of occupations. Concepts included are career environments, tools, uniforms, activities and titles.

VISUAL ENVIRONMENT

- Occupation and tool pictures (Peabody Kit — Level 2)
- Mount magazine pictures on 9" x 12" construction paper of people in different occupations.
- Hang up the Occupation Interviews when they are returned from home (see Home Projects).
-
-
-
-

DISPLAYS

- **Tools Display:** Tools from different occupations (carpenter, doctor, chef, electrician, teacher, artist, etc.) may be displayed and talked about. Use a few each day or all at one time.

- **Hats Display:** Baseball cap, Army hat, clown hat, cowboy hat, fire-fighter's hat, king's crown, hard hat, waiter's hat, etc.; these can be used for improvisations and discussion.

-

MATERIALS

- Career Environment Cards (Developmental Learning Materials)
- Occupations Match-Ups (Developmental Learning Materials)
- Career Awareness Stickers (Communication Skill Builders)
- Occupation Crossword Puzzles, Community Helper Crossword Puzzles (Ideal)
- Make "Who Would Use A . . ." charts with names of tools. Have the students determine who would use each tool and explain what it would be used for (flashlight, wrench, hose, whistle, palette, test tube, gavel, binoculars, scale, etc.). This is a good activity for introducing new vocabulary in context.
- *Perceive and Respond: Sounds Related to Tools* — tape (Modern Education Corporation)
- Mix and Match Puzzles — Occupations (Trend)
-

ACTIVITIES FOR LEARNING CONCEPTS AND LISTENING

- Talk about occupations of parents and friends. Then go through the occupation pictures and discuss them, the tools used, locations of jobs, training needed, and so on. Start with the most familiar ones first.

- Take a trip to the school office and ask the secretary to talk about her job. You could also ask the custodian, principal, nurse, and other personnel to explain theirs.

- Have older students interview school personnel or parents using the tape recorder.

- Act out (verbally or nonverbally) occupations.

- Make shoe box movies showing a day in the life of a worker. The students can narrate their stories.

- Write short descriptions of jobs on index cards. Students pick a card and match it with a corresponding picture. You may code the backs for self-checking.

- Talk about kinds of buildings where people work. List them on a chart (courtroom, restaurant, concert hall, studio, observatory, stadium, garage).

- Talk about inventors and their inventions (Alexander Graham Bell, Benjamin Franklin, the Wright Brothers, Henry Ford, etc.). Have the students draw and tell about their inventions (see LRE, List 97).

HOME PROJECTS AND FIELD TRIPS

- Talk about your occupation. Take your child to your place of business if possible. Let him take a tool that you use in your job to school to talk about. Help him fill out the Job Interview sheet.

- Take a trip to the fire station or another neighborhood business and talk to the employees about their jobs.

- Look in your garage, storeroom or toolroom for various kinds of tools and discuss them.

- Act out occupations with your child, or play "Descriptions": each person describes an occupation — location, uniform, tools, duties. Others guess the occupation.

BOOKS AND PHONOGRAPH RECORDS

Books

- *Little Monster's Neighborhood* by Mercer Mayer (Random House).
- Sesame Street *People In Your Neighborhood* (Golden Shape Book).
- *Busy Day — Busy People* by Tibor Gergely (Random House).
- *At Work* by Richard Scarry (Golden Press).
- *Who Runs the City* by Hildebrandt (Platt and Munk).
- *The Best Word Book Ever,* section on occupations (Golden Press).

Interview

1. What is your occupation (job)?

2. Where do you work? (Kind of building, vehicle, etc.)

3. What do you do?

4. What tools do you use? (calculator, wrench, etc)

5. What do you like best about your job?

SKILLS LISTS

Phonology, Morphology, Syntax

- Display the occupation pictures with the labels attached. Ask the students to find all the one-syllable worker names, then two, and so on. (See vocabulary list for names.)

    1-syllable words: chef, clown
    2-syllable words: soldier, waitress

- Check other units for activities in this category.

Rhyming Sentences (LRE, Lists 1–2)

The sailor left his *coat* on the *boat.*
The chef will *bake* a chocolate *cake.*
The vet gave the dog a *shot* that hurt a *lot.*
The man who will *dance* wears black *pants.*
The reporter writes *down* what's happening in *town.*
The cleaners got the *dirt* out of your new *shirt.*
The pretty *nurse* has a new *purse.*
Billy will *stop* at the barber *shop.*
Jan broke her *arm* working on the *farm.*
My sister *Sue* got a job at the *zoo.*

Scrambled Sentences (LRE, Lists 15–16)

3 Words
the where's hospital
money bankers like
lives save lifeguards
get waitresses tips
paints Juan pictures

4 Words
clowns people laugh make
brave must be explorers
very surgeons intelligent are
plumber is a Billy
designs houses an architect

- Have the students make up more scrambled sentences about occupations pictures.

Sentence Types

Hospital

The doctors are very friendly here.	(declarative)
Have you ever been in a hospital?	(interrogative)
My arm is hurt!	(exclamatory)
Take me to the hospital.	(imperative)

- Other subjects for mini-books: *army, police station, cartoonist.*

Question Game

Answers: the post office   (**Question:** *Where* do you buy
                                              stamps?)

          a tour guide
          on a boat
          a hammer
          she designs buildings
          a garbage truck
          a detective
          with scissors and a comb
          on a farm
          with a fancy camera
          a bible

- One student selects an occupation card. The others ask her questions to find out her line of work. Put up a question word chart to help them (how, where, what, do, can, is, when).

Semantics

Homonyms (LRE, Lists 23–26)

- See vocabulary list.

Compound Words (LRE, List 83)

- Ask the students to name occupations that are compound words. Give clues. For example:

  A person who lays bricks.   bricklayer
  A person who fights fires.   firefighter
  A person who sells things.   salesperson

  Consult the vocabulary list for other compound words.

- Have the students make up new names, such as:

  A person who cuts meat.   meatcutter
  A person who fixes shoes.   shoefixer
  A person who writes books.   bookwriter

Scrambled Sentence Sequence (LRE, Lists 41–42)

The robber went into the bank.	1
The police came and arrested him.	3
He stole some money.	2
They jumped over a fence.	3
The horse started to run.	2
The jockey got on her horse.	1
The farmer took the eggs to market.	3
The hens laid eggs.	1
The farmer took the eggs from the nests.	2
He pulled my tooth.	3
I had a toothache.	1
I went to the dentist.	2
The forest ranger looked through binoculars.	1
He saw some smoke.	2
He called the firefighters.	3

Incomplete Sentences (LRE, Lists 43–46)

The doctor put a cast on my l_____ .

Jim makes pizzas at a r_____ .

The policeman made an a_____ .

The cartoonist draws pictures for the n_____ .

The car salesman makes commercials for t_____ .

Mr. Booker solves mysteries; he is a d_____ .

The florist makes beautiful b_____ .

The accountant uses a c_____ .

- Explain unfamiliar words.

Cognitive Tasks

Analogies (LRE, Lists 52–62)

A *hoe* is to a *gardener* as a *spatula* is to a _____ .   cook

An *apron* is to a *waitress* as a *costume* is to a _____ .   clown

Clay is to a *potter* as *material* is to a_____ .   seamstress

A *song* is to a *musician* as a *joke* is to a _____ .   comedian

Chopping is to *butcher* as *preaching* is to _____ .   minister

Laboratory is to *scientist* as *studio* is to _____ .   artist

Stadium is to *football player* as *highway* is to ____ .   bus driver/ policeman

Garage is to *mechanic* as *hospital* is to _____ .   nurse/ doctor

Dancer is to *leotard* as *soldier* is to_____ .   uniform

- Help students make up other analogies.

Classification (LRE, Lists 65–68)

zookeeper, trainer, veterinarian	accountant
waitress, cook, manager	florist
judge, courtroom, lawyer	author
sailor, captain, soldier	announcer
priest, minister, rabbi	coach
bank, theater, library	stadium
hammer, saw, screwdriver	carpenter
hospital, clinic, doctor's office	church
baker, chef, cook	restaurant

- Make a classification chart to fill in. Examples:

who	does what	where	with
architect	designs homes	studio	T-square
coach	teaches sports	gymnasium	whistle

Do this as an individual, group or family activity.

Categories (LRE, Lists 63–64)

Outdoor jobs
Tools used by a construction worker
Workers in a hospital
Tools a homemaker uses
Occupations involved in news media
Things you would see in a mine
Workers who give talks or lectures
Workers who fix things
Workers who usually wear hats

Part-Whole Relationships (LRE, Lists 69–70)

- Remind students that the following are related to jobs.

A *stage* is part of a _____(theatre)_____ .

A *hose* is part of a ___(gas pump/fire truck)___ .

Shelves are part of a _____(library)_____ .

A *siren* is part of a ___(police car/fire truck)___ .

Keys are part of a ___(typewriter/piano)___ .

An *aisle* is part of a ___(supermarket/store/church)___ .

A *blade* is part of a ___(lawnmower/razor)___ .

Bleachers are part of a ___(stadium/gym)___ .

Associations (LRE, Lists 71–73)

Job
paycheck	timeclock	vacation
layoff	promotion	boss
interview	manager	wage
hire		

Airport
ticket booth	luggage	runway
passengers	stewardess	pilot
airplanes	gift shop	

- Other subjects: *lifeguard, courtroom, scientist.*

- List worker titles on a chart. Make a set of cards with job locations printed on them. Each student draws a card and matches it with the corresponding worker.

musician	concert hall	nurse	hospital
scientist	laboratory	artist	studio
pilot	airplane	secretary	office
teacher	classroom	umpire	stadium
usher	theater	waiter	restaurant
ranger	forest	grocer	store
judge	court	singer	nightclub
king	palace	professor	university

- Play "Who Will Help Me?" Each student draws a card with a task on it and asks "Who will help me . . .?"

. . . make a cake   . . . mail a package
. . . fix my car   . . . fly a plane

The student who answers must pantomime the action or explain how will he will help.

Similarities–Differences (LRE, Lists 74–76)

geologist–archaeologist	clothes designer–dressmaker
model–actor	scientist–pharmacist
forest ranger–farmer	reporter–journalist
library–bookstore	theater–church
house painter–artist	airport–train station

Inferences (LRE, Lists 78–79) See instructions, Unit 1.

I entertain people.   magician
I do not sing.
I mystify my audience.

I am involved in a professional sport.   referee
I work on a field.
I blow a whistle.

I usually become well-known.   politician
I am a public speaker.
I run for public office.

I work in a restaurant.   waiter/waitress
I walk a lot.
I take orders from customers.

I work indoors.   homemaker
I work with children.
I clean the house and make meals.

- Have the students make up some riddles about occupations. Evaluate their sets of clues; then use the riddles with other students.

Production of Language

Nonverbal (LRE, List 83)

- Show word or picture cards of occupations to the students. Let them pantomime the jobs, depicting the location, tools used and duties performed. The students may do them in pairs for practice in interaction; for an alternate activity, have them add dialogue.

Descriptions

- Let the student put on a hat from the occupation hats display. He then tells what he does all day in that job. Add actions. Other students may ask him questions.

Storytelling

- Let each student choose a hat story shape made from construction paper. Have him dictate a story about what he wants to be when he grows up. Print it on the shape. After displaying it, send it home for the parents to read and save. Let the older students read their stories on videotape and play back for evaluation of articulation, fluency, inflection, etc.

Short Talks (LRE, Lists 91–95)

- Give a talk on how to do something; for example:

    How to Tend a Garden
    How to Lay Bricks

- Take one object from the display. Describe it in detail.

- Interview someone for a job as a _____(choose occupation)_____ .

- Give a commercial for a dishwashing school.

- Give a commercial for a paintbrush that paints without paint.

- Give a report on a famous inventor.

- Give an on-the-spot report about the Wright Brothers' first flight.

- Interview Betsy Ross, the flagmaker.

Improvisations (LRE, Lists 87, 96)

- You are a lumberjack cutting down a tree when it suddenly looks as if it will fall on you.

- You are a hair stylist. You are cutting someone's hair when you find out it is a wig!

- You are a dentist. You are trying to fix a little child's teeth, and he won't stop crying.

- You are running a game show on television. Show what happens with your contestants.

- Act out a courtroom scene.

- Show pictures of groups of people at work. Let small groups of students make up dialogue and act out what they think may be happening or will happen.

Story Shape

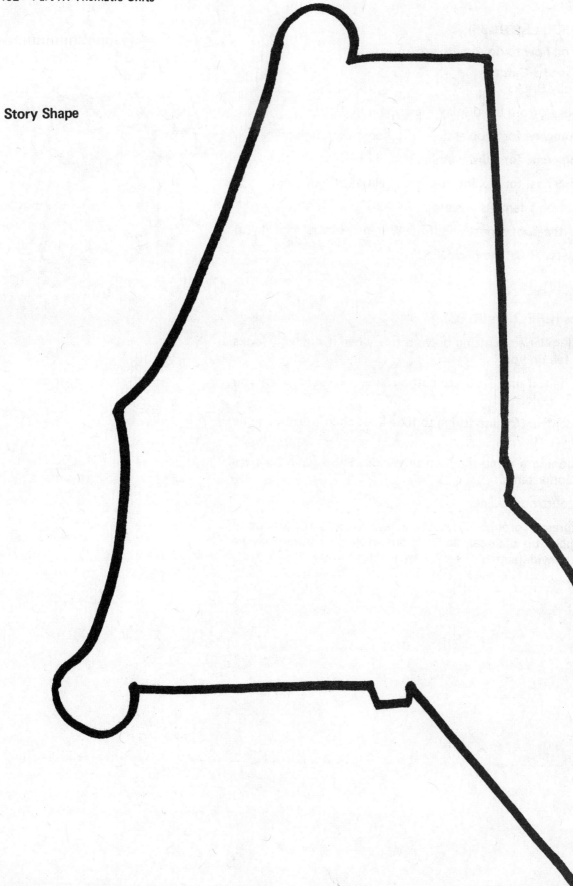

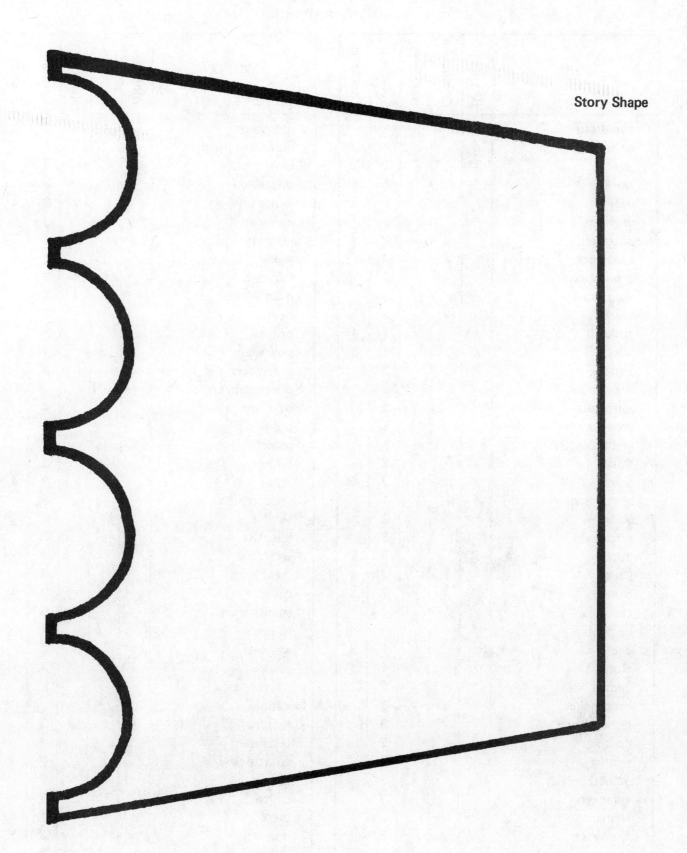

Story Shape

VOCABULARY LIST

WORD	Rhyme	Compound	Homonym	Syllables	Phonemes
Occupations					
occupation				4	
job	✓			1	3
work				1	3
tool	✓			1	3
uniform				3	
paycheck		✓		2	
timeclock		✓		2	
promotion				3	
vacation				3	
layoff		✓		2	
strike	✓		✓	1	4
boss	✓			1	3
athlete				2	
announcer				3	
astronaut				3	
architect				3	
archaeologist				5	
artist				2	
actor				2	4
astronomer				4	
barber				2	
bricklayer		✓		3	
butcher				2	4
baker				2	4
banker				2	
custodian				4	
carpenter				3	
chef				1	3
clown	✓			1	4
cashier				2	
dressmaker		✓		3	
dishwasher		✓		3	
doctor				2	
dentist				2	
detective				3	
engineer				3	
farmer				2	
firefighter		✓		3	
grocer				2	
homemaker		✓		3	
judge	✓			1	3

WORD	Rhyme	Compound	Homonym	Syllables	Phonemes
lifeguard		✓		2	
librarian				4	
lawyer				2	
mapmaker		✓		3	
miner (minor)			✓	2	4
musician				3	
mechanic				3	
model			✓	2	4
minister				3	
maid (made)	✓		✓	1	3
painter				2	
printer				2	
politician				4	
pharmacist				3	
photographer				4	
psychologist				4	
pilot				2	
reporter				3	
referee				3	
sailor				2	4
salesperson		✓		3	
soldier				2	
scientist				3	
secretary				4	
technician				3	
usher				2	3
veterinarian				6	
waiter				2	
waitress				2	
zookeeper		✓		3	
Locations					
factory				3	
restaurant				3	
courtroom		✓		2	
airport		✓		2	
office				2	
bank	✓		✓	1	4
hospital				3	
library				3	
store	✓		✓	1	4
market				2	

VOCABULARY LIST

WORD	Rhyme	Compound	Homonym	Syllables	Phonemes
garage				2	
zoo	✓			1	2
stadium				3	
mine	✓		✓	1	3
farm				1	4
nursery			✓	3	
home	✓			1	3
highway		✓		2	
route (root)	✓		✓	1	3
forest				2	
vehicle				3	
church				1	3
school				1	4
indoor		✓		2	
outdoor		✓		2	

WORD	Rhyme	Compound	Homonym	Syllables	Phonemes
Other:					

UNDERSEA TOUR CO.

UNIT 9
Transportation—Space

CONCEPTS

Unit 9 considers various modes of transportation and their uses, signs and their meanings, and exploration of space.

VISUAL ENVIRONMENT

- Space mural (see pages 158–160)
- Functional Signs (Developmental Learning Materials)
- History of Aviation, Historic Vessels, Railroading posters (Giant Posters, Inc.)
- Maps of space, the moon
- Other space posters
- Pictures of modes of transportation with labels

DISPLAYS

- **Transportation Display:** toy and model vehicles of all kinds (motorcycle, car, truck, wagon, bus, carriage, construction vehicles, and so on). The students may bring small vehicles of their own to add to the display.

MATERIALS

- Play Family Village (Fisher-Price) — This durable toy is very useful for eliciting contextual language about transportation. It includes different kinds of vehicles and is large enough for several students to use at one time for creative play.
- Transportation cards (Peabody Kit — Level 2)
- "Star Wars" trading cards
- Seals and stickers — signs and transportation (Dennison)
- *Perceive and Respond: Sounds of Transportation* — tape (Modern Education Corporation)
- Classification/Logical Order Picture Cards — vehicles (Milton Bradley)

ACTIVITIES FOR LEARNING CONCEPTS AND LISTENING

- Play a space sounds record as the children come in to introduce them to the space mural. Discuss space travel, the planets and our solar system.
- Brainstorm kinds of vehicles, categorizing them into: land vehicles, water vehicles, air vehicles. Compare, contrast, describe. Talk about the objects in the display.

Add: foil-covered cardboard stars, sponge or styrofoam balls for planets, a flag for the spaceman, glitter on space vehicles and model rockets.

- Talk about signs and their use and importance. Make construction paper signs for the students to take home and hang up (Keep Out, Danger, Quiet, My Room).

- Have the students select pictures from old travel magazines or brochures from a travel agency. Then they can give travelogues. Slides may be used if they have them at home. View Master reels or filmstrips provide interesting visual aids.

- Make category books with pictures of transportation and signs. This is a good project to continue at home. Keep the books on a young authors' table and use for other activities.

- Say the following nursery rhymes and songs with the children: "London Bridge Is Falling Down," "I Saw a Ship a–Sailing," "Rub-a-dub-dub, Three Men In a Tub," "There Was an Old Woman Tossed Up In a Basket," "Twinkle, Twinkle, Little Star." (Send home the words for a family activity.)

HOME PROJECTS AND FIELD TRIPS

- Help the child fill out the Transportation Survey Sheet (see page 162). Talk about when and where you have traveled on each kind of transportation. Send the survey back to school.

- Take a trip to the airport or train station. Discuss transportation and all that you see. (Provide on the home letter some ideas for discussion on the field trip.)

- Pantomime ways of traveling. Use the vocabulary list.

- Take a trip to the service station. Discuss the gas pumps, what the mechanics do, and look at the hydraulic lift and other interesting tools.

-

-

-

NOTES

TRANSPORTATION
HOW WE'VE TRAVELED

Kind of transportation	Student	Parents

SAMPLE LETTER

Dear Parents:

    Our language theme is <u>Transportation-Space</u>. Please help
your child learn new words and concepts by doing these activities:

HOME PROJECT AND FIELD TRIPS

    1. Help your child fill out the "Transportation--How
        We've traveled" sheet. Talk about when and where
        you went. Add more to the list and send it to school
        for your child to share.

    2. Go to the <u>airport</u> or <u>train</u> or <u>bus station</u>. Talk about
        what goes on there and what you see.

    3. Make a booklet of transportation. Cut pictures out of
        magazines or papers or help your child draw them and
        put them on the pages. Send it to school.

VOCABULARY

    Discuss the words on the attached list.

    Thanks for your help. Your child learns so much from you!

                Sincerely,

TRANSPORTATION VOCABULARY

AIR	WATER	LAND
helicopter	houseboat	ambulance
airplane	canoe	bicycle
hot-air balloon	kayak	bus
rocket	submarine	go-cart
hang glider	diving bell	skateboard
blimp	speedboat	stagecoach
tram	ship	fire engine
trapeze	raft	train
parachute	sailboat	tractor
ski-lift	sleigh	wagon
jet	skis	horse
magic carpet	yacht	elephant
		ostrich
		lunar rover

Talk about how they work, how they are alike and different, who would use them, where they go.

OTHER VOCABULARY:

propeller	anchor	license
countdown	oars	mechanic
takeoff	periscope	locomotive
pilot	harbor	caboose
control tower	pier	siren
rudder	compass	traffic
splashdown	sails	emergency
satellite	slopes	escalator

BOOKS AND PHONOGRAPH RECORDS

Books

- *The Best Word Book Ever,* sections on airplanes, cars, boats (Golden Press).

- *Away We Go* (Platt and Munk).

- *The Train Book* (Golden Press).

- *Charlie Brown's Third Super Book of Questions and Answers . . . about all kinds of boats and planes, cars and trains and other things that move!* (Random House).

- *What Makes It Go, What Makes It Work, What Makes It Fly, What Makes It Float?* by Joe Kaufman (Golden Press).

- *The Little Engine That Could* by Watty Piper (Scholastic Book Services).

- *The Sign Book* (Golden Press).

- *Never Pat a Bear: A Book About Signs* (Golden Press).

Records

- *The Planets* by Tomita (RCA).

- *Star Wars* (20th Century Records).

- *Bert and Ernie Sing Along* — "She'll Be Coming Around the Mountain," "Row, Row Your Boat," "I've Been Working On the Railroad" (Sesame Street).

- *Signs* (Sesame Street).

SKILLS LISTS

Phonology, Morphology, Syntax

- Beginning sounds: Make up space menus, using alliteration and adjectives; for example:

  Marvelous Martian macaroni
  Galactic green beans
  Huge heavenly hot dogs
  Lightweight lunar lambchops
  Weightless water
  Solar space soup

- Using the objects on the space mural or the vehicles in the transportation display, have the student name one item and tell the number of syllables in the word. Then tell one interesting fact about the item.

Rhyming Sentences (LRE, Lists 1-2) Make up more!

The rockets had a *race* in outer *space.*
Up on *Mars* they don't drive *cars.*
I have a toy *rocket* in my coat *pocket.*
The little *boat* would not *float.*
A big *plane* goes faster than a *train.*
Be careful when you *drive* if you want to stay *alive.*
We sang a *tune* by the light of the *moon.*
Bill fell off the *sled* and hit his *head.*
I walked in bare *feet* down the hot, hot *street.*
Did you have *fun* out in the *sun?*

Scrambled Sentences (LRE, Lists 15-16)

3 Words
is where Mars
brave are astronauts
rocketship crashed the
earth rotates the
bicycles ride kids

4 Words
in boat the get
stop the at stoplight
see I lighthouse a
Juan parachute opened the
the broken robot is

Sentence Types

- Make mini-books with one sentence and an illustration on each page.

  Go-Cart
I got a go-cart for my birthday.	(declarative)
Would you like a ride?	(interrogative)
It sure goes fast!	(exclamatory)
Fasten your seatbelt.	(imperative)

- Other subjects for mini-books: *skateboard, subway, Star Wars, Martians.*

Question Game

Answers: trapeze   (**Question:** *What* does a circus performer swing on?)

underground
float down the river
at the observatory
gravity
a U.F.O.
a siren
Evil Knievel
through a telescope
a stoplight

Semantics

Homonyms (LRE, Lists 23–26)

- See vocabulary list.

Antonyms (LRE, Lists 28–30)

bright–dull	sink–float
far–near	forward–backward
fast–slow	light–heavy
large–small	antique–modern
noisy–quiet	dangerous–safe
over–under	depart–arrive
stop–go	buy–sell
bumpy–smooth	nervous–calm

- Others:

Compound Words

- See vocabulary list.

- There are many compound words in this unit. Make two sets of word cards to be matched. For example:

  air — plane
  speed — boat
  take — off

- See LRE (Lists 21–22) for additional activities.

Basic Concepts and Following Directions (LRE, Lists 19–20, 47–49)

- Use the reproducible space map (page 168). Give directions to the students to follow, such as:

  "Draw a line from the rocket to the sun."
  "Color the sun yellow and put an X on the moon."

- Have one student give directions to another. Encourage specific language for directions. Record and listen to check accuracy.

Scrambled Sentence Sequence (LRE, Lists 41–42)

The skydiver pulled the ripcord.	3
He jumped out.	2
The skydiver opened the airplane door.	1
The alarm rang.	1
The firemen jumped on the truck.	2
They put out the fire.	3
Jose bought a ticket.	1
He went around and around.	3
He got on the ferris wheel.	2
He saw a new star.	2
The other scientists came to look.	3
The astronomer looked through the telescope.	1
The miners went underground.	1
They struck gold!	3
They worked for hours.	2

Incomplete Sentences (LRE, Lists 43–46)

Last night we saw a beautiful s_____ in the sky.

The rocket blasted off from the e_____ .

The satellite is in o_____ around the earth.

The ship came into the h_____ .

Did you get a t_____ for speeding?

My friend rides a u_____ .

The airplane landed on the r_____ .

The pirate ship s_____ in the ocean.

The baby went riding in his s_____ .

The pilot opened his p_____ .

■ Have the students think of several synonyms or appropriate words that could be filled in for each sentence. For example:

Last night we saw a beautiful (star, moon, cloud, shooting star, sky rocket, bird, sunset).

Cognitive Tasks

Analogies (LRE, Lists 52–62)

Steering wheel is to *car* as *handlebars* are to_____ .	bike
Bus is to *station* as *airplane* is to _____ .	airport
Bicycle is to *two* as *tricycle* is to _____ .	three
Hot air balloon is to *quiet* as *jet* is to_____ .	noisy
Moon is to *shine* as *stars* are to_____ .	twinkle
Microscope is to *scientist* as *telescope* is to _____ .	astronomer
Moon is to *planet* as *sun* is to_____ .	star
Scuba diver is to *wet suit* as *astronaut* is to _____ .	spacesuit
Day is to *light* as *night* is to _____ .	dark
Motor is to *speedboat* as *oar* is to_____ .	rowboat

Classification (LRE, Lists 65–68)

raft, ship, surfboard	camper
ambulance, fire engine, police car	taxi
scooter, bicycle, wagon	moped
elevator, escalator, merry-go-round	bus
star, sun, comet	planet
moon, crater, rocks	star
instruments, backpack, oxygen	countdown
telescope, binoculars, microscope	kaleidoscope
invent, design, build	robot
bright, shining, twinkling	star
car, truck, van	train

Categories (LRE, Lists 63–64)

Names of planets
Parts of a rocketship
Things an astronaut does
Characters in *Star Wars*
People who work in vehicles (pilot, chauffeur, sailor, etc.)
Kinds of street signs
Vehicles that don't have motors
Animals people can ride
Vehicles that go in the air

- Send the category list home with directions for a family game.

Part–Whole Relationships (LRE, Lists 69–70)

A *nose cone* is part of a ____(rocket)____ .

An *antenna* is part of a ____(satellite)____ .

"Four, three, two, one" is part of the ____(countdown)____ .

An *oar* is part of a ____(rowboat)____ .

A *periscope* is part of a ____(submarine)____ .

The *control tower* is part of the ____(airport)____ .

Handlebars are part of a ____(bicycle)____ .

A *lane* is part of a ____(highway)____ .

A *mast* is part of a ____(sailboat)____ .

A *caboose* is part of a ____(train)____ .

- Give the students clues if they need them.

- Select a vehicle from the display, and brainstorm the names of all the parts.

Associations (LRE, Lists 71–73)

Parachute

float	airplane	jump
land	ripcord	pilot
clouds	rocketship	sky
emergency	skydive	

Sleigh

Santa Claus	reindeer	one horse
jingle bells	snow	Rudolph
runners	cold	

- Other subjects: *traffic, astronaut, UFO, gravity.*

- Make mobiles or collages and stories to go with them.

- Play "How Would You Go?" As you name a place, the students must name the modes of transportation they would use to get there. For instance:

> through a jungle (vine, jeep, elephant)
> down a river (canoe, kayak, motorboat)
> to the moon
> to the top of a skyscraper
> to the bottom of a snow-covered hill
> to a friend's house
> to the bottom of the ocean
> through a tunnel
> in a parade
> to the top of a telephone pole
> (See LRE, List 158 for places.)

Similarities-Differences (LRE, Lists 74-76)

kayak-rowboat	taxi-bus
ambulance-fire engine	satellite-spaceship
carriage-covered wagon	astronomer-astronaut
stop light-stop sign	Big Dipper-Milky Way
baby buggy-tricycle	umbrella-parachute

- Others:

Inferences (LRE, Lists 78-79)

I am a planet.   Venus
I am bigger than the Earth.
I have lots of moons.

I have an interesting occupation.   astronomer
I work in an observatory.
I study the stars.

I am a vehicle made of metal.   wagon
I do not have a motor.
Children sit in me.

I am driven fast.   fire engine
I make a special kind of noise.
I am used in emergencies.

I have three colors.   stop light
I light up.
People stop or go when they see me.

Several people can ride in me.   elevator
I am usually indoors.
I go up and down.

- Help the students make up others.

Logical Sequences (LRE, List 80)

- Present the words in each set in random order. Have the students rearrange them in logical order.

moon–Earth–star–solar system	(size)
Mercury–Earth–Mars–Pluto	(distance from sun, or size)
countdown–blastoff–flight–splashdown	(time sequence)
canoe–sailboat–yacht–ship	(size)
tricycle–go-cart–car–race car	(speed)
unicycle–bicycle–tricycle–wagon	(number of wheels)

Production of Language

Nonverbal (LRE, List 85)

- Have students pantomime means of transportation. They may then build short skits or improvisations around each transportation word.

Descriptions

- Have the students describe one object from the display table. Other students guess the object.

Storytelling (LRE, List 90)

- Cut out ship story shapes. Let each student dictate to you an adventure story or a story about a trip (real or imaginary). If appropriate, have the students act out the story at a later time. Seeing his own story come to life is very exciting for a student. Similarly, he may use it for a flannel board story.

- Invite parents to come in for reading, dramatization or telling of student stories.

- Start a story for the students. When you point to a student, he must continue the story.

    I went outside one night. I saw a flying saucer floating above my house and . . .

    My uncle gave me a robot for my birthday. It could . . .

I looked through a giant telescope. To my surprise I saw a . . .

I was on a safari in Africa. I was riding an elephant and . . .

I jumped out of an airplane and opened my parachute. Then a strange thing happened . . .

Short Talks (LRE, Lists 91–95)

- How to launch a hot-air balloon.
- The dangers of skateboarding.
- Interview Santa Claus about his transportation.
- Give an on-the-spot report of the blastoff of a moon rocket.
- Give a commercial for a bicycle that can fly.
- Give a commercial for a modern covered wagon.
- Give a commercial for a new robot that does your homework.
- Interview an alien who has landed on Earth. Find out what kind of music, clothes, food and entertainment it likes.
- Tell what the Earth will be like in 100 years.

Improvisations (LRE, Lists 87, 96)

- You are a cab driver at rush hour in New York. A person in a hurry gets into your cab.
- It is the year 2010. Get in your mini-rocket and show us where you go.
- You are a miner working underground. All of a sudden you see something surprising!
- You and your friend get stuck in an elevator. Show us what you do.

Questions and Discussion Topics

- Why do stars twinkle?
- Why is the sky blue?
- Where does gasoline come from?
- What is an anchor for?
- Are flying saucers real?
- Suggest some questions in the home letter, for dinner table discussion topics. There are many good questions in *Charlie Brown's Third Super Book of Questions and Answers*.

Story Shape

VOCABULARY LIST

WORD	Rhyme	Compound	Homonym	Syllables	Phonemes
Air Transportation					
transportation				4	
vehicle				3	
airplane		✓		2	
jet	✓			1	3
helicopter				4	
blimp				1	
parachute				3	
seaplane		✓		2	
runway		✓		2	
takeoff		✓		2	
airport		✓		2	
hangar (hanger)			✓	2	
pilot				2	
passenger				3	
propeller				3	
Water Transportation					
boat	✓			1	3
canoe				2	4
houseboat		✓		2	
speedboat		✓		2	
sailboat		✓		2	
rowboat		✓		2	
ship	✓			1	3
kayak				2	4
raft				1	4
yacht	✓			1	3
submarine				3	
schooner				2	
harbor				2	
pier (peer)	✓		✓	1	3
deck	✓		✓	1	3
lighthouse		✓		2	
voyage				2	
ferry (fairy)			✓	2	4
sled	✓			1	4
sleigh (slay)	✓		✓	1	3
snowmobile		✓		3	
dogsled		✓		2	
snowplow		✓		2	
iceskate		✓		2	

WORD	Rhyme	Compound	Homonym	Syllables	Phonemes
Rail Transportation					
railroad		✓		2	
roundhouse		✓		2	
caboose				2	
engine				2	
station				2	
train	✓		✓	1	4
tracks	✓		✓	1	
fare (fair)	✓		✓	1	3
carriage				2	
coach			✓	1	3
Land Transportation					
ambulance				3	
bus				1	3
racer				2	
taxi				2	
van	✓			1	3
bicycle				3	
wagon				2	4
scooter				2	
subway				2	
freeway		✓		2	
sidewalk		✓		2	
highway		✓		2	
stoplight		✓		2	
road (rode)	✓		✓	1	3
alley				2	3
street	✓			1	
avenue				3	
drive				1	4
speed	✓			1	4
sign	✓		✓	1	3
bridge				1	4
skateboard		✓		2	
wheelchair		✓		2	
unicycle				4	
elevator				4	
escalator				4	
monorail				3	
moped				2	
tank	✓		✓	1	4

VOCABULARY LIST

WORD	Rhyme	Compound	Homonym	Syllables	Phonemes
Land (continued)					
caution				2	
danger				2	
yield	✓			2	4
slow	✓			1	3
curve				1	3
Space					
rocket				2	
spacesuit		✓		2	
liftoff		✓		2	
countdown		✓		2	
splashdown		✓		2	
weightless		✓		2	
nosecone		✓		2	
spacecraft		✓		2	
space	✓		✓	1	4
star	✓		✓	1	4
planet				2	
galaxy				3	
atmosphere				3	
moon				1	3
sun (son)	✓		✓	1	3
sunlight		✓		2	
orbit				2	
sunspot		✓		2	
starlight		✓		2	
gravity				3	
comet				2	
launch			✓	1	4
fuel	✓			1	3
missile (missal)			✓	2	
capsule			✓	2	
flight	✓			1	4
oxygen				3	
astronomer				4	
scientist				3	
crew	✓			1	3
captain				2	
altitude				3	
explore				2	
shine	✓			1	3

WORD	Rhyme	Compound	Homonym	Syllables	Phonemes
twinkle				2	
sky	✓			1	3
crater				2	
alien				3	
observatory				5	
gas	✓			1	3
Other:					

UNIT 10
Communications

CONCEPTS

Unit 10 is concerned with many types of communication: body language, verbal, written, pictorial, sound and symbolic communication. Much of this material is especially appropriate for students above grade 3.

VISUAL ENVIRONMENT

- Sign language or deaf alphabet cards
- Alphabet charts
- Samples of hieroglyphics, picture writing, and writing in other languages
- Book jackets (ask your librarian)
- History of the Telephone poster (telephone company)
- Pictures of television personalities
- Make a news Bulletin Board. Students may bring in articles or pictures to talk about and hang up under the proper labels:

  Sports   Animals   Weather   People

-
-
-
-

DISPLAYS

- **Communications Display:**
  Auditory: telephone, telegraph set, radio, tape recorder, records, hearing aid, television, whistle, bell

  Visual: newspaper, magazine, books in other languages, poster, photographs, bumper sticker, campaign button, printing set, teletype sample (from newspaper office), flags

  Other: Braille sample, watch, thermometer

- **Books Display:** comic book, flip book, miniature book, pop-up book, scratch and sniff book, poetry book, dictionary, encyclopedia, atlas, thesaurus, novel, biography, ABC book, etc. Also include books children make up themselves.

-

-

MATERIALS

- *Password* (Milton Bradley)
- *Scrabble* and *Scrabble for Juniors* (Milton Bradley)
- *Silly Syntax* (Houghton Mifflin)
- Rhyming cards and games (Developmental Learning Materials, Teaching Resources, Trend, and others)
- Tape recorder and video tape recorder
- Toy telephones
-
-
-

NOTE: Recommend to the parents such word games as *Scrabble* and *Password* for family play.

ACTIVITIES FOR LEARNING CONCEPTS AND LISTENING

- Make up a television show. Tape record or video tape it and play back for students and/or families and class.

- Discuss newspapers. Put out a small newspaper composed by the students.

- Practice making calls with telephones (emergency, information, ordering, etc.).

- Listen to tapes of different languages. Also look at foreign books. Talk about the differences in languages.

- Put on plays or puppet shows. The students may make up their own scripts or improvise dialogue.

- Play word games with the students.

- Recite poems, tongue twisters, jokes, etc.

- Talk about and demonstrate sign language and Braille.

- Discuss the different kinds of books in the book display. Have the students bring in their favorite books from home to add to the display and talk about these.

- Make up a classification chart of student favorites including favorite book, television show, movie, song, magazine.

- Talk about how books are written and made. Invite an author in to share her experiences. (See *Where Everyday Things Come From*, sections on Paper and Books.)

- Have each student make a mini-book to add to the book display.

- Talk about items in the communications center. Compare, contrast, and talk about their use in communication.

- Visit the school or public library.

-

HOME PROJECTS AND FIELD TRIPS

- Visit the Post Office and talk about what goes on there: the jobs of the postal workers, what happens to letters and packages, the use of mail boxes, stamps. Also look at and use the stamp dispensers and change machines.

- Help your child write a letter and mail it.

- Visit the public library and help your child apply for a library card if she does not have one. Tour the library, explaining about the different sections. Make regular trips to check out books.

- Help your child start his very own library. Give books as gifts, surprises and rewards for him to keep and cherish.

- Order a child's magazine for your child and use it with him each month. (Teacher: See section on Books for titles to suggest to parents.)

- Tour a newspaper office or television station.

- Use a bulletin board for family messages and communications. Write notes to your child often (e.g., "I love you," "Thanks for helping me today," "Please clean your room," "There is a surprise for you in the cookie jar!")

- Set aside time to talk to and listen to your child every day. Share your dreams, experiences, problems, plans, and ideas.

NOTES

BOOKS AND PHONOGRAPH RECORDS

Books

- *Telephones. Writing. Television.* Wonder Books (Grosset and Dunlap).

- *Edward Lear's Nonsense Book* (Dover Publications).

- *Writing* (the history of) by Ellen Dolan (McGraw–Hill).

- *Where Everyday Things Come From* (Platt and Munk).

- *What Makes It Go, Work, Fly, Float,* sections on television, radio, movies, printing press, etc. (Golden Press).

- *The Mammoth Book of Word Games* by Richard B. Manchester (Hart Publishing Co., Inc.).

Suggested Magazines

(NOTE: See Appendix B for publishers' addresses.)

- *Dynamite.* (Interesting facts, fiction, activities and visual material.) Grade level: 3–6.

- *Electric Company.* Children's television workshop. Grade level: 1–6.

- *Sesame Street.* Grade level: K–1.

- National Geographic *World* (about nature, people, places, events. Includes activities, posters, collectors' cards.) Grade level: 1–6.

SKILLS LISTS

Phonology, Morphology, Syntax

- See *The Mammoth Book of Word Games* for communication activities which develop these skills.

- Use the rhyming object set (see Appendix A). Have each student find a set of rhyming objects and make up a sentence. "The *bear* sat on the *chair."*

- For a more advanced activity, use another set of objects. Each student selects an object, thinks of a rhyming word, and creates a sentence.

- Make up mini–commercials using rhyming words and the students' names:

soap	Don't give up *hope.* Use Uncle Mac's *Soap.*
house	Every intelligent *mouse* buys an Acme *house.*
bank	Bring your money to Wilson's *Bank* and you'll have yourself to *thank.*
car	Make a wish upon a *star,* and buy a Johnny Little *car.*

Students may make posters for their products and put on a television sales show for another group.

Rhyming Sentences (LRE, Lists 1–2)

Please take a *look* at my comic *book.*
We walked down the *trail* to get our *mail.*
I can see the *stamp* by the light of the *lamp.*
Your writing was *better* when you wrote that *letter.*
Please do not *screech* when you give a *speech.*
Don't lay the *poster* on the *toaster.*
You hear a dial *tone* on the *telephone.*
When he saw the *ad,* my *dad* got *mad.*

Scrambled Sentences (LRE, Lists 15–16)

3 Words
funny commercials are
letter this mail
watch cartoons I
a poem write
change the channel

4 Words
play disc jockeys records
filming is the camera
reporter a is Al
the President talking is
telegram Anita got a

Sentence Types

Pony Express

The Pony Express delivered mail.	(declarative)
Did you get a letter?	(interrogative)
Wow! The horses go fast!	(exclamatory)
Don't lose this postcard.	(imperative)

- Other subjects: *commercials, sign language, cartoons.*

Question Game (See instructions in Unit 1.)

Answers: a headline   (**Question:** *What* do you call the title
of a newspaper story?)

in a dictionary
the comics
the Morse Code
the story of someone's life
a commercial
makes announcements
in a studio
pantomime
"Lights, camera, action!"

Semantics

Homonyms (LRE, Lists 23–26)

- See vocabulary list.

Compound Words (LRE, Lists 21–22)

- See vocabulary list.

Basic Concepts and Following Directions (LRE, Lists 47–49)

- Give two students identical sets of objects (large and small blocks, car, pencil, animal, etc.). With a screen between them, one student gives directions to the other for setting or arranging the objects in a pattern identical to the one he is making. Tape record the instructions for checking the giving and following of directions.

Scrambled Sentence Sequence (LRE, Lists 41–42)

The director starts filming a television show.	1
The director says "Cut!"	3
The actor makes a mistake.	2
You answer the telephone.	2
The telephone rings.	1
It is a wrong number.	3
He types the story.	2
A reporter goes to an accident.	1
The story is in the newspaper.	3
He delivers them to the homes.	2
The people read the papers.	3
The paperboy gets the papers.	1
The publisher prints the book.	2
An author writes a novel.	1
It is sold in bookstores.	3

Incomplete Sentences (LRE, Lists 43–46)

- Point to the initial letter of the missing word on an alphabet strip as you read the sentence.

My mom likes to read m_____ .

Who is the a_____ of *Cinderella?*

The reporter had a d_____ of 12 o'clock.

The disc jockey wears h_____ .

S_____ type letters.

Did you have your p_____ taken for the newspaper?

The actor read his lines from a s_____ .

"Peanuts" is a c_____ strip.

Please talk into the m_____ .

We mailed our l_____ .

Cognitive Tasks

Analogies (LRE, Lists 52–62)

Television is to *see* as *radio* is to _____ .   hear

Telegram is to *telegraph* as *printout* is to _____ .   computer

Pamphlet is to *thin* as *book* is to _____ .   thick

True is to *biography* as *make-believe* is to _____ .   novel

Editor is to *newsroom* as *producer* is to _____ .   studio

Headline is to *newspaper* as *title* is to _____ .   book

Camera is to *film* as *recorder* is to _____ .   tape

Advertisement is to *magazine* as *commercial* is to__.   television

Comic strip is to *pictures* as *paragraph* is to _____ .   words

Sign language is to *deaf* as *Braille* is to _____ .   blind

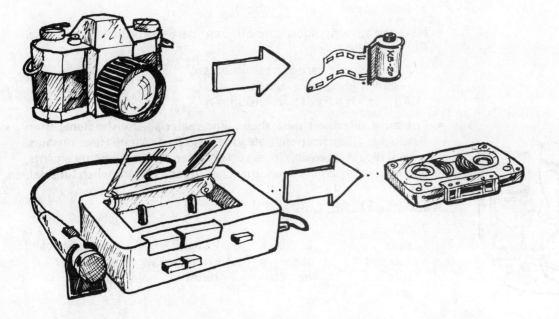

Classification (LRE, Lists 65-68)

biography, fable, poem	author
headline, comics, advertisement	reporter
lights, cut, action	director
postmark, stamp, address	letter
poster, bumper sticker, sign	announcement
lecture, monologue, speech	pantomime
producer, director, actor	television
title, index, chapter	book
antenna, channel, screen	radio
books, shelves, card file	librarian

Categories (LRE, Lists 63-64)

Kinds of books
Things in a television studio
Sections of a newspaper
Names of fairy tales
Things you can write with
People who work on a television show
Names of television programs
Things in a library

- Ask the students which television programs they watch regularly. List these on a chart and categorize them into types of programs.

Part-Whole Relationships (LRE, Lists 69-70)

An *antenna* is part of a ____(television set)____ .

A *lens* is part of a ____(camera)____ .

A *receiver* is part of your ____(telephone)____ .

A *headline* is part of a ____(newspaper)____ .

Keys are part of a ____(typewriter)____ .

A *camera person* is part of a ____(television crew)____ .

Books are part of a ____(library)____ .

E, F, and G are part of the ____(alphabet)____ .

Index is part of a ____(book)____ .

- Have the students substitute different part-words in each sentence. For example:

    An *antenna* is part of a television set.
    A *screen* is part of a television set.
    A *switch* is part of a television set.

- Put on a television quiz show. For material, use the items from Analogies, Classification, Categories and Part-Whole Relationships. Video-tape it if possible, make up commercials and announcements, and invite the parents or another class in for a viewing when finished.

Associations (LRE, Lists 71-73)

TV Show

stars	audience	camera	microphones
makeup	scenery	commercials	announcer
studio	nervous	rerun	director
props			

- Other words for association: *post office, reporter, Morse Code.* Select others from the vocabulary list.

Similarities-Differences (LRE, Lists 74-76)

- Select two teams of students, one for Similarities, one for Differences. After a word pair is presented, a student on the S team gives one similarity. Then a student on the D team tells a difference, and so on until a team cannot answer.

telephone-telegraph	radio-television
reporter-author	fiction-biography
dictionary-encyclopedia	lecture-conversation
sign language-Braille	magazine-newspaper
newsroom-studio	audio-video

Inferences (LRE, Lists 78-79)

I am a kind of book.   encyclopedia
There is a lot of information in me.
I have many volumes in one set.

I am a kind of writing.   Braille
I am made up of dots.
Blind people read me.

You see us on television.   puppets
Children especially like to watch us.
Someone else talks for us.

I play records.   disc jockey
I also talk a lot.
I am on the radio.

I am a kind of sign.   billboard
I am very big.
You see me along the highways.

Production of Language

Nonverbal (LRE, Lists 81-86)

- Brainstorm with the students all the body movements we use to communicate, such as waving for "good-by," nodding for "yes," and shrugging for "I don't know."

- Play "Charades" with the students to develop their body language skills. Use words from the vocabulary list as stimulus words.

Short Talks (LRE, Lists 91-95)

- Give a commercial for your favorite book.
- Interview another student pretending to be a famous person (an actor, author, character, etc.).
- Use a flannel board and tell a children's story.
- Use a puppet and tell some jokes.
- Read the comics as a radio show.
- Put on a news show and video tape it.
- Be a television reporter and give an on-the-spot report of a fire or other exciting event.
- Give a "You are There" program about a historical event. (See LRE, List 98, for suggestions.)

Improvisations (LRE, Lists 87, 96)

- You are cavemen who do not speak English. Use another language form to warn others a tiger is near.

- You take your little brother to the library. He makes a lot of noise and runs around. Show what you do.

- Dramatize making a television show (director, actors, sound engineers, film crew, etc.).

- You are a telegraph operator. You receive an incredible message. Show us what you do about it.

- You are a reporter assigned to a group of rock stars. Show us your interviews.

- Put on a television or radio show: news show, panel show, quiz show, talent show or short play. Let the students take responsibilities for directing, props, writing, taping, etc. Children who are seen by you individually or in small groups may tape separate segments. Then combine all parts for one show and show it to all the children.

- *Sprint* magazine has good plays suitable for fourth through eighth graders which may be used as radio shows to develop oral communication skills. Help the students select and develop sound effects to go with the script. Replay the show and listen for articulation, fluency, inflection and projection.

VOCABULARY LIST

WORD	Rhyme	Compound	Homonym	Syllables	Phonemes
Written/Printed					
communication				5	
message				2	
telephone				3	
telegraph				3	
teletype				3	
newsletter		✓		3	
newspaper		✓		3	
typewriter		✓		3	
newsroom		✓		2	
headline		✓		2	
proofread		✓		2	
deadline		✓		2	
reporter				3	
editor				3	
shorthand		✓		2	
advertisement				4	
interview				3	
book	✓			1	3
author				2	4
encyclopedia				6	
dictionary				4	
novel			✓	2	
poem				2	4
fiction				2	
biography				4	
fable	✓			2	4
research				2	
brochure				2	
pamphlet				2	
censor				2	
title				2	4
index				2	
photograph				3	
cartoon				2	
illustration				4	
poster				2	
sign	✓		✓	1	3
billboard		✓		2	
printout		✓		2	
Braille				2	
cursive				2	

WORD	Rhyme	Compound	Homonym	Syllables	Phonemes
manuscript				3	
alphabet				3	
magazine				3	
library				3	
tale (tail)	✓		✓	1	3
chapter				2	
Verbal/Nonverbal					
language				2	
speech	✓			1	4
lecture				2	
podium				3	
talk	✓			1	3
announcement				3	
speaker			✓	2	
microphone				3	
ventriloquist				4	
monologue				3	
pantomime				3	
charade				2	
Audiovisual					
script			✓	1	
commercial				3	
television				4	
channel			✓	2	
headphone		✓		2	
closeup		✓		2	
camera				3	
cue	✓		✓	1	2
action				2	
film				1	4
studio				3	
set	✓		✓	1	3
screenplay		✓		2	
sponsor				2	
station			✓	2	
program				2	
producer				3	
radio				3	
record			✓	2	
video				3	
zoom	✓			1	3

VOCABULARY LIST

WORD	Rhyme	Compound	Homonym	Syllables	Phonemes
Mail					
letter			✓	2	4
mail (male)	✓		✓	1	3
postcard		✓		2	
airmail		✓		2	
postmark		✓		2	
deliver				3	
stamp	✓		✓	1	
fragile				2	
mailbox		✓		2	

WORD	Rhyme	Compound	Homonym	Syllables	Phonemes
Other:					

UNIT 11
The Arts—Circus

CONCEPTS

Unit 11 surveys music, the visual arts and dramatic arts. The circus theme is also used for building language skills and vocabulary.

VISUAL ENVIRONMENT

- Pictures of clowns and circus performers mounted on construction paper
- Musical Instruments cutouts (Trend)
- Circus Bulletin Board cutouts (Dennison)
- Pictures of famous entertainers and artists
- Art prints
- Circus poster (Peabody Kit — Level K)

DISPLAYS

- **Music Display:** All kinds of musical instruments (toy or real), samples of music, metronome, conductor's baton. The instruments do not have to be in working order.

- **Art Display:** Samples of pottery, jewelry, macrame, painting, drawing, weaving, wood carving, chalk and watercolor, stitchery, illustrations, cartoons, pop art, sculpture, woodblock prints and collage. Also include materials used in these media.

- **Drama Display:** Masks, costumes, makeup, script, marionettes, puppets of all kinds. Collect hats (see "Materials" section).

MATERIALS

- All kinds of hats for creative drama (ask the PTA or parent helpers to collect or make them for you). Suggestions:

firefighter	cowboy	lady's fancy hat
policeman	top hat	ski mask
soldier	crowns	sombrero
clown	straw hat	beanie
witch	baker	pirate
hardhat	baseball cap	nightcap
sailor	bullfighter	bonnet
pilgrim	bridal veil	

- Circus seals (Dennison or Eureka) may be used for reinforcers or for making creative language games.
- Circus Time Finger Puppets (Trend)
- *Perceive and Respond: Sounds of Musical Instruments* — tape (Modern Education Corporation)
- Classification/Logical Order Picture Cards — instruments (Milton Bradley)

ACTIVITIES FOR LEARNING CONCEPTS AND LISTENING

■ Talk about musical instruments in the display and visual environment. Discuss similarities, differences, use, and sounds. Ask the band teacher if his students might demonstrate some of the instruments.

■ After discussing circuses, have the students put on a mini-circus with a ringmaster, magician, and performers. They may pantomime or improvise dialogue.

■ Discuss the forms of art in the display. Have each child demonstrate how to use one medium.

■ Make up and put on a melodrama.

■ Talk about artists, musicians, dancers, actors, and what they do. Invite one in to demonstrate (perhaps a parent).

■ Talk about different kinds of museums. Take a trip to one if possible. Make up mini-books as museum catalogs. For instance, a *Museum of Red Things:* find or draw pictures of lips, apple, cherry, blood, fire engine, stop light.

■ Read *Grover and the Everything in the Whole Wide World Museum* (Sesame Street book, Golden Press). Have the students guess what will be on each page.

■ Listen to and discuss the record, *A Child's Introduction to Melody and the Instruments of the Orchestra* (Walt Disney).

HOME PROJECTS AND FIELD TRIPS

■ Take a trip to a local art gallery or museum. Talk about what you see there.

■ Get a set of inexpensive watercolors; do a set of family paintings and hang them up in a home mini-gallery.

■ Save examples of your child's art work and stories each year in a permanent folder. Put the child's name and age on each piece.

■ Make a family movie or slide show.

■ Listen to records together and talk about the instruments you hear. Help your child identify different kinds of music: rock, classical, jazz, country-western, opera, musical comedy, etc.

■ Sing songs with your children: Christmas carols, songs from *Sesame Street* or other children's television programs, pop songs, folk songs, songs you remember from your own childhood. This helps your child improve memory, sequencing and language patterns.

■ Take your child to see a play. They are sometimes presented at local libraries, colleges or high schools, or community centers. Take him up to see the stage and actors afterward. (Specialist: Encourage the children to put on mini-plays at home for the family. Act out nursery rhymes or children's stories or make up skits.)

SKILLS LISTS

Phonology, Morphology, Syntax

- Direct the students' attention to the circus pictures in the visual environment. Use this stimulus for practicing articulation carry-over or syntactical and morphological forms in sentences.

> I see a clown spinning at the circus.
> The lion jump**ed** through the hoop.
> The monkey *is swinging* on the bar.
> *Who is* holding a chair?

Either have the students describe what they see, or you ask questions to elicit language structures.

Rhyming Sentences (LRE, Lists 1–2) Make up others.

> The dancing *girl* will try to *twirl.*
> My sister *sings* when the doorbell *rings.*
> In this *scene,* the villain is very *mean.*
> After the curtain *call,* meet me in the *hall.*
> The lions will *rage* inside the *cage.*
> The circus *bear* sat on a *chair.*
> The movie star has a fancy *car.*
> The artist does not *rush* when he paints with a *brush.*
> Will you *ask* to see the clown's *mask?*
> We waited all *day* to see a stage *play.*

Scrambled Sentences (LRE, Lists 23–26)

3 Words
ballet difficult is
bow take a
the applauded audience
paints the artist
funny talk puppets

4 Words
your put on makeup
lullaby a sing me
clowns up blow balloons
the beautiful is sculpture
starting is the concert

Sentence Types

Circus
I see the circus parade.   (declarative)
Did you watch the trapeze artist?   (interrogative)
She did a double flip!   (exclamatory)
Don't yell so loud.   (imperative)

- Other subjects: *clowns, jazz, dancing.*

Question Game

Answers:

a tutu	(**Question:** *What* kind of dress does a ballerina wear?)
at the box office	(where)
behind the camera	(where)
a trumpet	(what)
push down on the keys	(how)
the ringmaster	(who)
a comedy	(what)
after the performance	(when)
a marionette	(what)
cotton candy	(what)

Semantics

Homonyms (LRE, Lists 23–26)

- See vocabulary lists. Act out the pairs of words.

Antonyms (LRE, Lists 28–30)

- Find opposite concepts on the circus poster. Have the students make up sentences.

high–low	wild–tame
before–after	loud–soft
easy–hard	tragedy–comedy
light–dark	behind–in front
fast–slow	fat–skinny
expensive–cheap	graceful–clumsy
funny–sad	strong–weak

Compound Words (LRE, Lists 21–22)

- Discuss the meanings of the combined words. Make mix and match sets on index card strips.

- Use the words in a "round robin" story. Each child draws a compound word card and must add a sentence to the story using that word.

Basic Concepts and Following Directions (LRE, Lists 19–20, 47–49)

- Give each child a copy of the circus page (page 194). Give oral directions to be followed. For example:

  "Color the lion's nose red and his ears green."
  "Draw a line from the juggler to the ringmaster."
  "Make a flag under the clown."

Scrambled Sentence Sequence (LRE, Lists 41–42)

The painting is hung in the gallery.	3
He paints a beautiful picture.	2
Steven gets out his easel and brushes.	1
The tiger growled and chased the trainer.	3
The trainer opened the cage.	1
He snapped his whip.	2

POP!

Andy puts on his clown makeup.	1
He juggles and gives balloons to the kids.	3
He puts on his costume and goes onstage.	2
The orchestra plays the song.	3
The composer writes a song.	1
He makes many copies of the music.	2
The play begins.	1
The actors take a bow.	3
There is an intermission.	2

Incomplete Sentences (LRE, Lists 43-46)

The rock and roll band has two electric g_____ .

Is blue or yellow your favorite c_____ ?

The sculptor carved a beautiful s_____ .

We saw many paintings at the m_____ .

The artist will paint your p_____ .

There are many i_____ in the band.

The potter uses c_____ to make his pots.

We asked the movie star for his a_____ .

The ballet dancer s_____ around fast.

The u_____ will take you to your seat.

Cognitive Tasks

Analogies (LRE, Lists 52-62)

Camera is to *photographer* as *watercolors* are to
_____ .   artist

Weaver is to *loom* as *musician* is to _____ .   instrument

Laugh is to *comedy* as *cry* is to _____ .   tragedy

Lines are to *actor* as *notes* are to _____ .   singer

Tutu is to *ballerina* as *costume* is to _____ .   actor

Keys are to *piano* as *strings* are to_____ .   guitar

Beat is to *drum* as *blow* is to _____ .   horn

Gallery is to *painting* as *theater* is to _____ .   play/movie

Composer is to *music* as *author* is to _____ .   book

Pick is to *banjo* as *strum* is to_____ .   guitar

Classification (LRE, Lists 65-68)

trapeze, lion, ringmaster	dentist
stage, set, theater	bedroom
painter, sculptor, weaver	butcher
easel, potter's wheel, loom	piano
stilts, trapeze, bicycle	growling
hymn, tune, melody	concert
trumpet, trombone, flute	drum
composer, author, musician	auditorium
tent, auditorium, theater	performers
cotton candy, hot dog, popcorn	coke

Categories (LRE, Lists 63-64)

Circus animals
Instruments that you blow
Kinds of music
Things used to make pictures
Movements a ballet star makes
People that work in a theater
Things you eat at a circus

Part-Whole Relationships (LRE, Lists 69-70)

A *note* is part of a _____(scale/song)_____ .
A *mouthpiece* is part of a _____(horn)_____ .
A *stage* is part of a ____(theater/auditorium)____ .
A *clown hat* is part of a _____(costume)_____ .
A *trunk* is part of a ____(circus elephant)____ .
A *person* is part of an _____(audience)_____ .
A *keyboard* is part of a _____(piano)_____ .
A *singer* is part of a _____(chorus)_____ .
A *musician* is part of an ____(orchestra/band)____ .

Similarities-Differences (LRE, Lists 74-76)

violin–guitar	rehearsal–performance
chalk–pencil	mask–makeup
painting–drawing	puppet–marionette
tightwire–trapeze	circus–carnival
gymnast–ballerina	lion–tiger

Associations (LRE, Lists 71-73)

▪ List the words on a chart to be used in composing circus stories.

Circus

lion	ringmaster	balloons
ring	clown	popcorn
tent	trapeze	juggling
flags	elephant	sawdust
stilts		

Bands

march	instruments	rock and roll
notes	music	uniform
loud	drum	leader

▪ Other subjects: *mask, museum, painting.*

Inferences (LRE, Lists 78–79)

I like music.	conductor
I help others play instruments better.	
I direct a group of musicians.	
I am an instrument.	piano
I am very big.	
I have 88 keys.	
I perform in the circus.	elėphant
I am very large.	
I have a trunk.	
I am a large building.	theater
I have lots of seats.	
I am used for plays.	
I am made by an artist.	statue
Sometimes I look like a person.	
I am made of hard material.	

Production of Language

Nonverbal (LRE, Lists 81–86)

- Have the students pantomime using musical instruments after you have discussed each one. They may also pantomime using different types of art media. Do frequent demonstrations for them.

- Pantomime different circus characters. Then improvise dialogue to go with each one and create skits. Invite the families in to see the informal show.

Storytelling

- The students may dictate circus stories to be written on the tent story shapes. These stories may be used for improvisation by small groups. Flannel board or puppet characters may be made to present the stories to younger children.

  SAMPLE STORY:
  Once there was a little chubby clown named Sam. Now Sam wasn't an ordinary clown. He was famous. Everybody thought he was the best clown because he did tricks no other clown could do. One day when Sam was doing tricks he fell and broke his arm. It really was just one of his tricks and everyone laughed.

  One day he really did fall and break his arm. Everybody thought it was just a trick. So Sam never went into the clown business again.

  by Lila (grade 4)

  (The students talked over her story and made a mini-play out of it which they presented to a kindergarten class.)

Short Talks (LRE, Lists 91–95)

- Give a commercial for a mask that changes you into a celebrity.

- Give a commercial for a paint brush that paints without paints.

- Give a commercial for clothes that make you invisible.

- Interview Charlie Chaplin or Marcel Marceau.
- Demonstrate with visual aids how to draw, paint, sculpt or weave.
- Be a circus barker and introduce different acts.
- Tell how to tame a circus lion or teach an elephant to do tricks.

Improvisations (LRE, Lists 87, 96)

- You are a clown getting ready to go under the Big Top for a performance. But you have a problem. Show us what it is.
- You are a band director. You always hear one sour note from your band. Do something about it.
- You are the strong man in the circus. The crowd is waiting for you to lift an enormous weight — but you can't do it.
- You are on a roller coaster for the first time. You are very scared and want to get off.
- You are giving a piano concert. Someone in the audience keeps coughing very loud. It annoys you. What will you do?
- Think up other ideas with your students for improvisations concerning the Arts or Circus.
- Each improvisation idea may be used several times. Each group of students will give different interpretations.
- The students may put on a magic show. Encourage the families in the home letter to help their children learn magic tricks. Video tape the show if possible and show it to the parents. Even if only a few parents attend your plays, displays, story-telling sessions or video tape showings, the experience is rewarding for the students and helps build self-confidence.

Story Shape

Making animal hats....

1. Trace pattern onto colored paper. Flop design over to make a mate to match

2. Draw in "fur" with a marker. Add a touch of pink chalk or crayon inside the mouse and rabbit ears

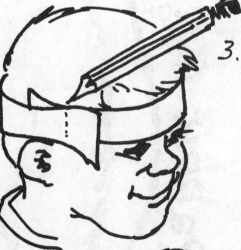

3. Cut a 2" strip of the same color paper, long enough to wrap around the child's head with a few inches of overlap.

4. Staple the headband with the sharp points facing outward. Staple on the ears, sharp points out.

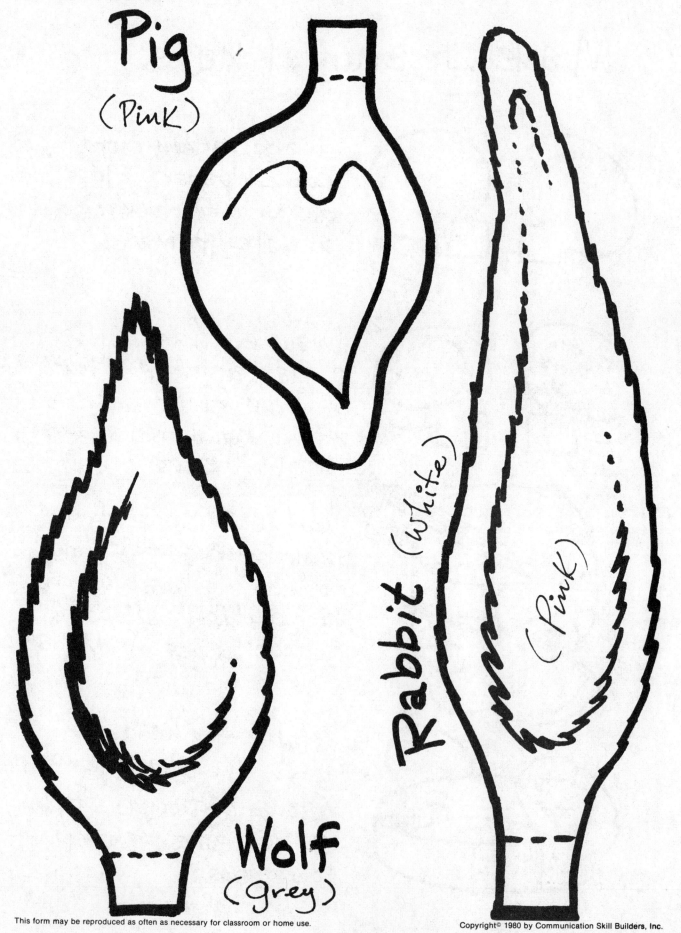

Pig
(Pink)

Wolf
(Grey)

Rabbit (white)

(Pink)

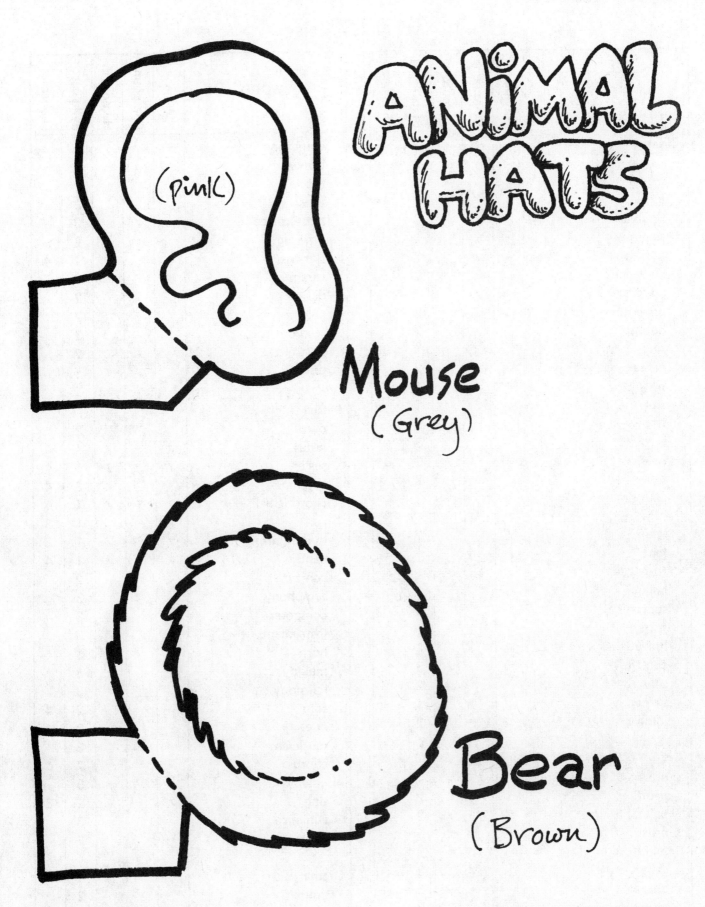

ANIMAL HATS

Mouse
(Grey)

Bear
(Brown)

(pink)

VOCABULARY LIST

WORD	Rhyme	Compound	Homonym	Syllables	Phonemes
Circus					
circus				2	
clown	✓			1	4
juggle				2	4
ringmaster		✓		3	
sideshow		✓		2	
tightrope		✓		2	
bareback		✓		2	
sawdust		✓		2	
popcorn		✓		2	
hotdog		✓		2	
ring	✓		✓	1	3
parade				2	
trick	✓			1	4
stunt				1	
trapeze				2	
acrobat				3	
net	✓		✓	1	3
trainer				2	
animals				3	
cage	✓			1	3
whip	✓			1	
tent	✓			1	4
flag	✓			1	4
balloon				2	
souvenir				3	
stilts				1	
brave	✓			1	4
colorful				3	
silly				2	4
striped				1	
midget				2	
Art					
art	✓			1	3
painting				2	
palette (palate)			✓	2	
brush	✓			1	4
sculpture				2	
gallery				3	
display				2	
museum				3	

WORD	Rhyme	Compound	Homonym	Syllables	Phonemes
exhibition				4	
canvas				2	
easel				2	
artist				2	
masterpiece		✓		3	
drawing				2	
sketch				1	4
ceramic				3	
design				2	
color				2	
studio				3	
portrait				2	
print			✓	1	
Music					
music				2	
notes	✓		✓	1	4
scale	✓		✓	1	4
rhythm				2	4
chord (cord)	✓		✓	1	4
jazz				1	3
hymn (him)	✓		✓	1	3
band	✓		✓	1	4
concert				2	
symphony				3	
composer				3	
instrument				3	
horn	✓		✓	1	4
melody				3	
harmony				3	
solo				2	4
duet				2	4
musician				3	
chorus				2	
lullaby				3	
sing	✓			1	3
audience				3	
applause				2	
Drama					
drama				2	
play	✓		✓	1	3

VOCABULARY LIST

WORD	Rhyme	Compound	Homonym	Syllables	Phonemes
act			✓	1	3
scene (seen)	✓		✓	1	3
tragedy				3	
comedy				3	
theater				3	
star	✓		✓	1	4
rehearsal				3	
costume				2	
makeup		✓		2	
bow	✓		✓	1	2
backdrop		✓		2	
upstage		✓		2	
actress				2	
standin		✓		2	
spotlight		✓		2	
stagehand		✓		2	
autograph				3	
scenery				3	
usher				2	
puppet				2	
marionette				4	
mask				1	4
celebrity				4	
Dance					
dance				1	4
ballet				2	4
tutu				2	4
practice				2	
spin	✓			1	4
twirl	✓			1	4
leotard				3	
slipper				2	
intermission				4	
ticket				2	

WORD	Rhyme	Compound	Homonym	Syllables	Phonemes
Other:					

UNIT 12
Monsters—Fantasy—Storytelling

CONCEPTS

Unit 12 uses familiar and imaginative literature to encourage creative language skills in the students. Spontaneous verbal and body language are developed through student story-telling and creative drama.

VISUAL ENVIRONMENT

- Nursery Rhymes Bulletin Board cutouts (Trend, Eureka)
- Fairy Tale Bulletin Board cutouts (Trend)
- American Folklore Bulletin Board cutouts (Trend)
- Large "I Wonder" posters (Peabody Kit — Level 3)
-
-

DISPLAYS

- **Storytelling Display:** Puppets representing characters from familiar stories. Add to the display puppets the students make.

  Have a parent-child workshop after school and make simple puppets such as those shown below. (Note: make three holes in the back of the burger carton for two fingers and thumb to open and close mouth. Make slits in tennis balls ahead of time. Have scraps of colored paper and other materials ready to use for faces and decorations.) Use the puppets for mini-shows.

- **Fantasy Display:** Toy robots, fantasy figures. The students may wish to bring some from home to tell about and add to the display.

- **Book Display:** All kinds of fairy tale, nursery rhyme and fantasy books. Include special ones like pop-ups, miniatures, mix-n-match books, giant books, and books students have made. Use them for special activities and leisure reading.

Paper Cup   Tennis Ball   Burger carton

MATERIALS

- Nursery rhyme pictures (GOAL — Milton Bradley)
- Flannel Board Fairy Tales (Milton Bradley)
- Once Upon a Time finger puppets (Trend)
- Seals — Fairy Tale, Nursery Rhyme, American Folklore (Eureka)
- See-quees story boards — Fairy Tales (Judy)
- Viewmaster reels and projector — fairy tales
- Materials for puppet making
- Simple costumes and props

ACTIVITIES FOR LEARNING CONCEPTS AND LISTENING

- After discussing different kinds of monsters and listening to stories from books or on records, have the children describe their favorite monsters (appearance, what he eats, does, where he lives, etc.).

- Have students make up news articles (complete with headlines) for a newspaper or radio show about nursery rhyme or fairy tale incidents (LRE, Lists 99, 100). Make up a small newspaper with the stories and have the students take copies home.

  ### EGGMAN CRACKS UP
  Last night a large eggman named Humpty Dumpty fell off the city wall. The royal horses and soldiers were called to rescue him. They worked for three hours to repair his cracks but could not put him together again. He is still in the city hospital.
  by Amy (grade 4)

- Students may practice telling fairy tales with flannel board characters or puppets. The stories may be presented for younger children or parents or may be video taped.

- The students may act out (improvise) nursery rhymes, fairy tales, folklore or their own stories. This is a good time to read many of these stories and talk about the characters and events, and increase appreciation of our literary heritage. Dress up as a fictional character when you read that book!

- Students may use See-quees boards to sequence stories and retell them.

HOME PROJECTS AND FIELD TRIPS

- Encourage the parents to read to their children every night. Suggest appropriate books and give demonstrations of how to talk about, read, and ask questions about books. Parents appreciate this help. Assure them that children should still be read to *after* they learn to read.

- Also advise parents to tell stories to their children. Encourage them to let the children join in and add to the stories (fairy tales, ghost stories, tall tales, ethnic stories, spontaneous stories, etc.).

- Invite the parents to come and watch some story improvisations.

BOOKS AND PHONOGRAPH RECORDS

Books

- *The Monster at the End of This Book* (Golden Press).
- *There's a Nightmare in My Closet* by Mercer Mayer (Dial Press).
- *Where the Wild Things Are* by Maurice Sendak (Scholastic Book Services).
- *Little Monster's Bedtime Book* by Mercer Mayer.
- *Giant John* by Arthur Lobel (Harper and Row).
- *Mix or Match Storybook* (Random House).
- *Poems to Read to the Very Young* (Random House).
- Books of fairy tales, nursery rhymes, fables and folklore.

Records

- *Mother Goose Nursery Rhymes* record (Disneyland).
- *Land of Giants,* folklore sung by the New Christy Minstrels (Columbia).
- *Thrilling, Chilling Sounds of the Haunted House,* good sound effects for ghost stories (Disneyland).
- *Sound-Ful,* sound effects (Golden Records).
- *Walt Disney's Best Loved Fairy Tales,* with book (Disneyland).
- *Monsters* — "Five Monsters In My Family," "I Want a Monster To Be My Friend," "Monster Lullaby" (Sesame Street).

SKILLS LISTS

Phonology, Morphology, Syntax

- For irregular verb practice, have each student tell what a storybook character *did*. You may wish to select certain characters to elicit the forms you are working on. Students may pick word cards or pictures of the characters or you may ask such questions as:

  "What did Snow White *bite* into?"
  "Snow White *bit* a poison apple."

  "What did Bo Peep *lose?*"
  "She *lost* her sheep."

  "What did the giant *say?*"
  "He *said,* 'Fee, Fi, Fo, Fum!'"

- Have the students retell fairy tales for articulation carryover practice.

- To practice initial consonant sounds, have the students help you compose tongue twisters about monsters or fantasy characters. The students may then practice saying them.

  A gory ghost gobbled gooey gumdrops.
  The rickety robot rattled rapidly.
  One wicked witch wanted a wonderful wand.

- See LRE, Lists 99 and 100, for names of fictional characters.

Rhyming Sentences (LRE, Lists 1–2)

I know a *witch* who lives in a *ditch*.
Sally saw a *troll* that lives in a *hole*.
Phil saw a *mummy* who has a fat *tummy*.
The cute little *fairy* ate a *cherry*.
The dragon has a *tail* that's sharp as a *nail*.
Little Bo *Peep* went to *sleep*.
Jack *Sprat* wears a funny *hat*.
The monster with the *scar* got into the *car*.
Captain *Hook* learned to *cook*.
The witch made some *brew* to give to *you*.

Scrambled Sentences (LRE, Lists 15–16)

3 Words
roared the giant
diets Jack Sprat
wings have fairies
are dark dungeons
hairy Wolfman is

4 Words
under bridges live trolls
fire a breathes dragon
the wind howling is
nightmare had a I
the scared me monster

Sentence Types

Haunted House

We saw a huge haunted house.	(declarative)
Did you go in?	(interrogative)
A ghost said "Boo!"	(exclamatory)
Stay away from it.	(imperative)

- Other subjects: *Peter Pan, giants, Friday the 13th.*

Question Game

Answers: under the bridge   (**Question:** *Where* does a troll live?)

     in his castle
     on Halloween night
     Raggedy Ann
     King Kong
     fangs
     a dragon
     at midnight
     a cauldron
     a haunted house

- Help the students make up questions about fictional characters or stories. Create a quiz show and use the questions.

"Who lost her slipper at midnight?"
"Where did Humpty Dumpty sit?"
"When does Santa Claus come?"

- You may wish to give each student the list of question words and the list of characters to help them create questions.

Semantics

Basic Concepts and Following Directions (LRE, Lists 19-20, 47-49)

- Give each student a dittoed monster story shape.

- Give directions for drawing a face on one side.

"Make a big yellow nose in the center."
"Draw a shaggy brown beard on his chin."
"Draw five pointy white teeth in an orange mouth."

Compare the drawings to see if they are alike.

Idioms, Proverbs and Similes (LRE, List 99)

- Give the students a list of storybook characters. Have them make up *similes* for each one:

naughty as Peter Rabbit
small as Tom Thumb
floppy as Raggedy Ann
jolly as King Cole

Scrambled Sentence Sequence (LRE, Lists 15-16)

She ran away.	3
Miss Muffet was eating.	1
A spider came.	2
Cinderella lost her slipper.	2
She married the prince.	3
Cinderella went to the ball.	1
The mad scientist made a monster.	1
He scared people in the town.	3
The monster woke up.	2
Jerry knocked on the door.	2
Jerry went to the haunted house.	1
A ghost scared him.	3
Santa Claus came down the chimney.	3
He packed his sleigh.	2
Santa Claus hitched up his reindeer.	1

- Have the students make up sequence sets from fairy tales or nursery rhymes.

Incomplete Sentences (LRE, Lists 43-46)

The robot makes strange n_____ .

The dragon lived in a c _____ .

Cinderella lost her s _____ at the ball.

The sphinx is in the country of E_____ .

The w_____ rode a broom.

The wicked queen gave Snow White an a_____ .

The e _____ help Santa Claus.

Peter Rabbit almost got caught in the g_____ .

The m_____ does magic tricks.

Humpty Dumpty f_____ off the wall.

The Cartoon Game

- Cut out pictures of comic strip and storybook characters and glue them on white index card halves. On colored index card halves print a phrase that would correspond to each character, such as "eats spinach" or "quacks a lot." Play matching games with the cards to determine sentence sense.

    "Three pigs . . . build houses."

Cognitive Tasks

Analogies (LRE, Lists 52-62)

Captain Hook is to *ship* as *Yankee Doodle* is to __ .   pony

Red Riding Hood is to *wolf* as *Miss Muffet* is to__ .   spider

Mummy is to *tomb* as *king* is to _____ .   castle

Santa Claus is to *Christmas* as *ghosts* are to _____ .   Halloween

King Kong is to *hairy* as *dragon* is to _____ .   scaly

Snow White is to *Queen* as *Hansel and Gretel* are to
_____ .   witch

Three Pigs are to *wolf* as *Three Billy Goats* are to
_____ .   troll

Rip Van Winkle is to *20 years* as *Sleeping Beauty*
is to _____ .   100 years

Cinderella is to *slipper* as *Bo Peep* is to_____ . sheep

Elf is to *small* as *giant* is to_____ .   big

- Help the students make more of these analogies. Let the children
  take them home to quiz their families.

Classification (LRE, Lists 65–68)

Cinderella, Snow White, Sleeping Beauty   Rumplestiltskin
Peter Rabbit, Chicken Little, Dumbo   Peter Pan
gigantic, huge, monstrous   tiny
Frankenstein, Dracula, Wolfman   King Kong
growl, roar, snarl   squeak
teeth, fangs, tail   Dracula
elf, fairy, gnome   giant
Miss Muffet, Bo Peep, Jack Sprat   Cinderella
haunted house, castle, mansion   dungeon
make-believe, fictitious, mythical   true

Categories (LRE, Lists 63–64)

Characters in nursery rhymes
Animals in fairy tales
Things in a haunted house
Parts of a castle
Costumes for Halloween
Noises monsters make
Things that scare people
Words to describe Frankenstein

Part-Whole Relationships (LRE, Lists 69–70)

A *dungeon* is part of a _____(castle)_____ .

Fangs are part of _____(Dracula)_____ .

Squeaking door is part of a ___(haunted house)___ .

Wings are part of a ___(fairy)___ .

A *long nose* is part of ___(Pinocchio)___ .

A *throne* is part of a _____(castle)_____ .

A *peg leg* is part of ___(Captain Hook)___ .

Tricks are part of a _____(magic show)_____ .

Very big ears are part of ___(Dumbo/Bugs Bunny)___ .

Yellow feathers are part of _____(Chicken Little/Big Bird)_____ .

Associations (LRE, Lists 71–73)

Cinderella

pumpkin   coach   glass slipper
stairs   prince   godmother
mouse   midnight   wedding

- Other subjects: *mad scientist, nightmare, Pinocchio.*

Similarities-Differences (LRE, Lists 74-76)

elf–troll	king–prince
cat–bat	Jack Horner–Miss Muffet
cauldron–bowl	mummy–ghost
castle–cottage	howl–roar
Santa Claus–Easter Bunny	Snow White–Sleeping Beauty

Inferences (LRE, Lists 78-79) See instructions in Unit 1.

I am a nursery rhyme character. I am an old king. I have three fiddlers to entertain me.	Old King Cole
I am a scary creature. I live under a bridge. I know three billy goats.	troll
I am a building. I have many rooms. Kings live in me.	castle
I am a big animal. I am not real. I breathe fire.	dragon
I am a very strong man. I am in a tall tale. I chop down trees.	Paul Bunyan

- Make up more using local folklore.

Production of Language

Nonverbal (LRE, Lists 81-86)

- Students may pantomime nursery rhyme, storybook or cartoon characters. Others guess who they are. Talk about using facial expressions to show emotions and body movements to convey messages.

Storytelling

- Have a monster and ghost story contest. Set the mood by playing a haunted house record and telling ghost stories. Dress up in a costume that day. Read some monster stories (see Book List). Then encourage each child to dictate or write an imaginative story and illustrate it. Give every child a prize in some category (scariest, funniest, best ghost, best monster, etc.). Stickers on construction paper awards make good prizes.

- You may wish to help the students make plays out of their stories for dramatization. For example, this one was composed by a first grader:

> Once upon a time a monster and I went somewhere. Everybody was afraid of him. I told them, "Don't be afraid of him." Then the cops came and put him in jail. They didn't want him in town. When they were asleep, I took the keys and opened the door and my monster and I got away. The next morning when the policemen woke up, they found out we had escaped. We never went outside again.
>
> by Sam (grade 1)

As I read the student his story, he composed the lines for his play as follows:

Sam: Hey, monster, let's go outside and play. Put your coat on.

People: Look at that monster! He's really scary!

Sam: Don't be afraid of him. He won't hurt you.

Police: We are going to take your monster to jail. He is scaring all the people. We don't want him in our town.

Sam: Please don't take my monster!

Police: Okay, monster, get in this cage. Now, all the people will be safe.

Sam: I'm going to sneak in and get the keys and get my monster out. (goes in) Come on, monster, be quiet. We'll go home and lock the door.

Police: (Yawns) It's morning already. Hey, the monster's gone! Everybody look for him. We can't find him. They've escaped.

Sam: Be really quiet, monster. We will have to stay in this house for the rest of our lives. We'll just have to learn to be happy in here.

- Use the monster story shapes for the stories (page 214).
- Make up other fantasy stories. Make creative books and put them in the library to be read by others.

Short Talks (LRE, Lists 91–95)

- Tell a ghost story.
- Describe a monster for others to draw. Use a picture or your imagination.
- Make up a tall tale.
- Interview Robinson Crusoe on his island about his living conditions.
- Be Peter Piper and give a commercial for pickled peppers.
- Be Rip Van Winkle. Tell how it felt to come back after twenty years of sleeping.
- Give a hidden-camera on-the-spot report of Santa Claus getting ready to leave the North Pole on Christmas Eve.
- Have a panel discussion about nutrition with these characters: Miss Muffet, Jack Sprat, Peter Piper, Winnie the Pooh, Goldilocks, Johnny Appleseed.
- Have the students dress up as main characters of books they have read and give creative oral book reports.

Improvisations

- Do group improvisations of fairy tales, tall tales, myths, fables, ghost stories, or students' stories.

Story Shape

VOCABULARY LIST

WORD	Rhyme	Compound	Homonym	Syllables	Phonemes
Characters					
ghoul	✓			1	3
monster				2	
giant				2	
witch	✓			1	3
dragon				2	
troll	✓			1	4
gnome	✓			1	3
fairy (ferry)	✓		✓	2	4
elf				1	3
creature				2	
robot				2	
mummy	✓			2	4
ghost	✓			1	4
goblin				2	
king	✓			1	3
queen	✓			1	4
prince				1	
princess				2	
Dracula				3	
Frankenstein				3	
skeleton				3	
King Kong				2	
Description					
scary	✓			2	
tiny				2	4
huge				1	3
gigantic				3	
strange				1	
creaky				2	
ugly				2	4
toothy				2	4
scaly				2	
hairy	✓			2	4
bumpy				2	
wicked				2	
vicious				2	
horrible				3	
colorful				3	
weird				1	4
mysterious				4	

WORD	Rhyme	Compound	Homonym	Syllables	Phonemes
strong	✓			1	
fantastic				3	
noisy				2	4
haunted				2	
beautiful				3	
gory				2	4
Noises					
howl	✓			1	3
groan (grown)			✓	1	4
snarl				1	
cry	✓			1	3
growl	✓			1	4
scream	✓			1	
roar	✓			1	
wail	✓			1	3
cackle				2	
chuckle				2	
giggle				2	
hiss	✓			1	3
Parts					
claw	✓			1	3
horn	✓		✓	1	4
teeth				1	3
scar	✓			1	4
tail (tale)	✓		✓	1	3
fang	✓			1	3
scales			✓	2	
wings	✓			1	4
Other					
magic				2	
spell	✓		✓	1	4
potion				2	
brew	✓			1	3
cauldron				2	
night (knight)	✓		✓	1	3
Halloween				3	
moon	✓			1	3
midnight				2	
nightmare		✓		2	

VOCABULARY LIST

WORD	Rhyme	Compound	Homonym	Syllables	Phonemes
Other (cont.)					
imagination				5	
superstition				4	
fantasy				3	
castle				2	
cave	✓			1	3
graveyard		✓		2	
tombstone		✓		2	
dungeon				2	
rhyme	✓			1	3
tale (tail)	✓		✓	1	3
storybook		✓		3	
folklore		✓		2	
fable	✓			2	4
myth				1	3

WORD	Rhyme	Compound	Homonym	Syllables	Phonemes

PART III

Appendices

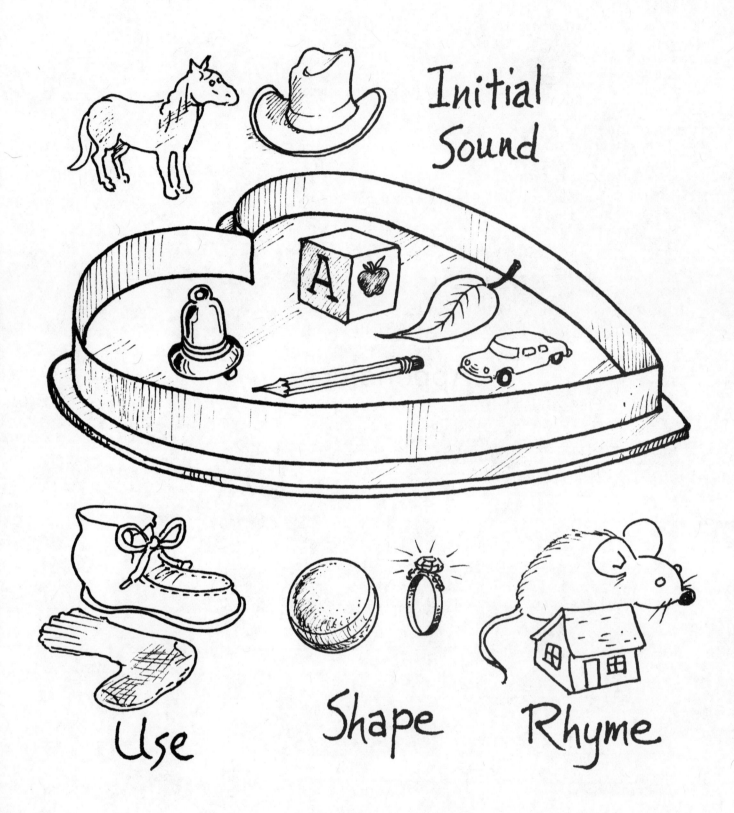

Initial Sound

Use

Shape

Rhyme

Object Collections

The following pages suggest kinds of items to collect for different skills practice. Any group of objects may be used for categorizing, syllabication, describing, or making up sentences or riddles. Some of the objects can easily be made (for example, flag, crown, fan). Store the objects in small shoe boxes which are labeled with the category name for easy retrieval.

Students of all ages are interested in the object collections and eagerly look forward to using them. The items suggested are inexpensive and easy to find. For example, you may use:

> birthday favors
> holiday favors (Halloween pumpkin, Santa Claus, skeleton, flag, bunny, etc.)
> doll clothes and furniture
> plastic foods
> ornaments
> plastic letters and numbers
> household items
> play money
> small musical instruments
> plastic animals
> miniature items
> small food packages (raisins, salt, candy boxes, etc.)
> parts of games
> old toys
> small prizes or cereal giveaways
> small objects in classroom (crayons, paper clips, etc.)
> old jewelry

Use objects for:

1. beginning sounds and sound discrimination games (also digraphs and blends). Place objects beginning with each letter or sound in strawberry baskets or cartons with the letter card attached on the front. Children can separate items into proper baskets. Start with two letters to discriminate, then three, four, and so on.

2. assembling groups of objects for practice in articulating a certain sound (initial /s/, final /s/, etc.) Use for word, phrase or sentence practice. These stimuli are much more interesting than pictures or word cards and elicit much more language.

3. preparing sets of objects for rhyming, compound words, irregular verb practice and comparison words (big-bigger-biggest, good-better-best, etc).

4. categorizing objects. Take any group of objects and have students group them according to one characteristic (soft, hard, round, red, etc.). Then group by two characteristics (soft and red, hard and brown).

5. associating objects. Assemble a group of objects in one box (use a Valentine heart-shaped box or a plastic pumpkin for added interest). The student picks two items and tells why they go together. The next student picks two more, and so on. This is a good cognitive game to demonstrate and recommend for family play.

6. making up riddles and giving clues about one object. Describe objects. Make up a story or a commercial about an object for oral communication practice.

OBJECT SETS

Rhyming

clamp-stamp-lamp
dice-rice
chick-stick
bag-rag-flag
mail-nail
chain-train
chair-hare/hair-bear
rake-snake-cake
thread-bed
jack-sack
lace-face
star-car
shell-bell
bed-sled
ear-deer
hen-pen
vest-nest
dime-lime
ring-string
chip-clip
tire-wire
skirt-shirt
boat-coat-goat
lock-sock-rock
book-hook
tool-spool
mop-stop
rose-nose-hose
cot-pot-knot
clown-crown

duck-truck
bug-rug
gum-drum
gun-sun
moon-spoon
house-mouse
can-man-fan
boy-toy
kitten-mitten
fox-box
bunny-money
rat-hat
bone-phone
heart-cart
fish-dish
_____
_____
_____
_____
_____
_____
_____
_____
_____
_____
_____
_____
_____
_____
_____

Compound Words

football
matchbook
suitcase
pipecleaner
motorcycle
keychain
golfball
grasshopper
seashell
teaspoon
pinecone
jumprope
mailbox
basketball

baseball
flashlight
clothespin
airplane
wastebasket
sunglasses
wallpaper
bankbook
billfold
toothbrush
sailboat
ragdoll
shoelace
butterfly

toothpick
newspaper
bandaid
wishbone
handcuffs
lipstick
ladybug
popcorn
cowboy
slingshot
bluebird
bookmark
cowbell
cufflink
cowgirl
earmuff
earphone
earring
fingerprint
highchair
lifesaver
lightbulb

noseplug
nutcracker
nutshell
paperback
raincoat
sandpaper
spaceman
spaceship
starfish
storybook
_____
_____
_____
_____
_____
_____
_____
_____
_____
_____
_____
_____

Irregular Verbs

beat — drum
bend — wire
bite — apple
blow — balloon
break — stick
build — blocks
burst — balloon
catch — ball
creep — mouse
cut — knife
dig — shovel
draw — pencil
drink — cup
drive — car
eat — apple
feed — spoon
fly — bird
give — present
go — man
grow — flower
hang — picture
hear — ear
lay — hen and egg
lie — man
light — candle
read — book
ride — horse/car
ring — bell
rise — sun
run — man

saw — saw
sew — needle and thread
shake — salt
shine — sun
shoot — gun
shrink — cloth
shut — box with lid
slide — sled
spend — coin
spin — top
spread — butter knife
stand — man
stick — stamp
sting — bee
strike — bat
sweep — broom
swim — fish
tear — paper
throw — ball
wear — doll
write — pencil
wind — yoyo
_____
_____
_____
_____
_____
_____
_____

Use a small bendable doll for:

bring	hold	make	speak
fall	is	run	stand
feel	keep	see	take
fight	kneel	sing	think
give	leave	sit	wake
hide	lose	sleep	weep

NOTE: Use the object and indicate the present form of the verb. "I *am bending* the wire. What did I do?"
Student: "You *bent* the wire."

"The man *is standing* on the table. What did he do?"
Student: "The man *stood* on the table."

Let the student perform the action and ask him what he did.

Initial Consonant Sounds

B	C	D	F
bug	comb	doll	fish
ball	curler	dollar	fork
bus	coat	dog	feather
balloon	camel	dinosaur	file
bottle	cow	deer	foot
boy	cowboy	duck	football
bear	car	domino	fox
bell	candy	dice	fan
bulb	card	dime	fire engine
book	candle	dish	four
box	cap	dirt	five
button	cat	dart	fur
battery	cork	daisy	face
baby	cup	devil	fence
bowl		donkey	father
bandaid			
barrette			
belt			
boot			
bed			
basket			

G	H	J	K
game	hat	jacket	kangaroo
gun	heart	jet	kitten
gum	head	jeep	king
goat	hand	jar	kite
girl	helmet	jumprope	kettle
gift	horse	jacks	key
guitar	house	jeans	
garbage can	horn	jelly beans	
ghost	hammer	jack o'lantern	
glove	hair	jewels	
glasses	hook	jug	
grapes	hen		
grass	handkerchief		
glue	harmonica		

L	**M**	**N**	**P**
lady	man	nest	pig
lizard	money	nail	pants
lipstick	motorcycle	nickel	pencil
lightbulb	marble	needle	pen
lion	mouse	napkin	penny
lace	monkey	newspaper	pepper
leg	matchbook	net	pot
lamb	measuring spoon	necklace	pipe
letter	mitten	nine	popcorn
lollipop	moose	nut	patch
ladder	map		purse
ladybug	magnet		pillow
lips	mirror		puppet
lamp	music		pan
lock			panda
lid			paint
leaf			

R	**S**	**T**	**V**
rock	salt	table	vase
rooster	soap	ticket	vest
rabbit	Santa	teeth	vacuum
rat	sign	tape	vitamins
ribbon	seal	turkey	valentine
rolling pin	sunglasses	turtle	violin
rocket	sucker	tiger	van
racer	soldier	tire	vine
record	sock	toothbrush	vampire
rubber band	six	tinker toy	
rhinoceros	seven	top	
ruler	saddle	two	
ring	sailboat	tool	
rope	scissors	tube	
rose	seed	toothpick	
raisins			

W	**Y**	**Z**
watch	yarn	zebra
wings	yoyo	zipper
worm	yardstick	zigzag
wire		zero
wagon		zipcode
woman		
wolf		
wax		
walrus		
wallet		
wishbone		
wastebasket		
witch		
window		
water		

Short Vowel Sounds

a	e	i	o	u
pan	thread	pig	pot	cup
bag	head	stick	block	rug
jack	egg	pin	mop	gun
caps	pen	clip	dog	duck
rat	leg	chick	box	brush
fan	vest	twig	lock	mug
man	nest	wig	rock	nut
crayon	peg	fish	sock	gum
ax	sled	dish	clock	bus
tack	net		cloth	bug
match	dress		frog	duck
bat	check			truck
apple				
hat				
lamp				
stamp				

Long Vowel Sounds

a	e	i	o	u
tape	seed	pipe	coat	tube
vase	bead	file	goat	cube
grape	sheep	sign	boat	tulip
lace	leaf	dime	bowl	uniform
rake	key	pie	soap	bugle
cape	bee	knife	comb	
ape	queen	kite	yoyo	
game	jeep	five	ghost	
face	teeth	prize	stone	
chain	tree	bike	rope	
snake			rose	
train			bone	

Blends and Digraphs

BL	CL	FL	GL	PL
block	clothespin	flashlight	glasses	plug
blanket	clip	flower	glass	plate
blouse	clown	flag	glove	plant
	clock		glue	
			globe	
			glider	

SK	SL	SN	SP	ST
skate	sled	snake	spider	star
skirt	slipper	snail	spoon	sticker
skunk	sleeve	snowman	sponge	stone
skeleton				stop sign
skull				

SN	SP	ST	SW	TW
snake	spider	star	swimsuit	twins
snail	spoon	sticker	swan	tweezers
snowman	sponge	stone	sweater	twenty
		stop sign		

SH	CH	TH	WH
shoe	chicken	thimble	whale
ship	chair	three	whistle
shell	cherry	thumb	wheel
shovel	chipmunk	thermos	wheelbarrow
shoehorn	check	thong	
sheep	church	thumbtack	
shirt	checker		
shorts	chapstick		
shampoo	chewing gum		

QU	CR	BR	GR
queen	crayon	bracelet	grass
quilt	crab	brush	grapes
quarter	crown	broom	groom
question mark	crib	bride	grasshopper
	cracker	bridge	
	cross	brick	
	crocodile		

FR	PR	DR	TR
frog	present	dragon	track
fruit	propeller	dress	train
frame	prize	drum	tree
	pretzel		truck
	princess		triangle
			trumpet

Comparisons

Collect several items in each category for practice in comparisons. For instance:

big-bigger-biggest/small-smaller-smallest
> pencils, cups, combs, spoons, toy cars, nails (three of each in varying sizes)

good-better-best/bad-worse-worst
> The same kinds of items may be used, but in varying conditions.

some-more-most/some-less-least
> marbles, crayons, plastic animals, cards, etc. (ten or more of each)

Opposites

boy-girl (dolls)
dirty-clean (cars)
happy-sad (faces)
little-big (spoons)
long-short (pencils)
new-old (toys)
slow-fast (bicycle and car)
young-old (dolls)
crooked-straight (sticks)

fancy-plain (material)
rough-smooth (materials)
thick-thin (books)
small-large (toys)
wet-dry (water and powder)
empty-full (containers)
closed-open (containers)
different-same (2 sets of objects)

APPENDIX B
Publishers of Materials

BOOKS

Abingdon Press
201 Eighth Avenue S.
Nashville, TN 37202

Crown Publishers
One Park Avenue
New York, NY 10016

Dial Press
1 Dag Hammarskjold Plaza
New York, NY 10017

Doubleday and Co., Inc.
501 Franklin Avenue
Garden City, NY 11530

Dover Publications
180 Varick Street
New York, NY 10014

Golden Press
Western Publishing Co., Inc.
Dept. M, 1220 Mound Avenue
Racine, WI 53404

Grossett and Dunlap
360 Park Avenue S.
New York, NY 10010

Harcourt, Brace, Jovanovich
757 Third Avenue
New York, NY 10017

Harper and Row
10 E. 53rd Street
New York, NY 10022

Hart Publishing Co., Inc.
15 W. 4th Street
New York, NY 10012

McGraw-Hill Publishers
1221 Avenue of the Americas
New York, NY 10020

Platt and Munk, Publishers
51 Madison Avenue
New York, NY 10012

Prentice-Hall, Inc.
Englewood Cliffs, NJ 07632

Random House
201 E. 50th Street
New York, NY 10022

Scholastic Book Services
904 Sylvan Avenue
Englewood Cliffs, NJ 07632

Charles Scribner's Sons
597 5th Avenue
New York, NY 10017

Western Publishing Co.
Dept. M, 1220 Mound Avenue
Racine, WI 53404

Whitman Books
Distributed by
Western Publishing Co.

Wonder Books
51 Madison Avenue
New York, NY 10010

MAGAZINES

Boys' Life
North Brunswick, NJ 08902

Dynamite
Scholastic Magazines, Inc.
50 W. 44th Street
New York, NY 10036

Electric Company Magazine
Children's TV Workshop
1 Lincoln Plaza
New York, NY 10023

Instructor Magazine
Post Office Box 6099
Duluth, MN 55806

Learning Magazine
1255 Portland Place
Boulder, CO 80302

National Geographic *World*
17th and M Streets, NW
Washington, DC 20036

Scholastic *Sprint*
902 Sylvan Avenue
Englewood Cliffs, NJ 07632

Sesame Street Magazine
North Road
Poughkeepsie, NY 12601

Sports Illustrated
541 N. Fairbanks Court
Chicago, IL 60611

PHONOGRAPH RECORDS

Buena Vista Records	Sesame Street
Columbia Records	20th Century Records
Disneyland	Walt Disney
MGM	Warner Brothers
RCA	(Order at your local record store.)

LEARNING MATERIALS

Communication Skill Builders, Inc.
Post Office Box 42050
Tucson, Arizona 85733

Dennison Manufacturing Co.
Framingham, MA 01701

Developmental Learning Materials (DLM)
7440 Natchez Avenue
Niles, IL 60648

Eureka
Dumore, PA 18512

Fisher-Price Toys
606 Girard Avenue
East Aurora, NY 14052

Giant Posters, Inc.
Box 406
Rockford, IL 61105

GOAL Language Development Kit
Milton Bradley
Springfield, MA 01101

Houghton-Mifflin
Palo Alto, CA 94304

Ideal School Supply Co.
Oak Lawn, IL 60453

Instructor Publications
Post Office Box 6099
Duluth, MN 55806

Judy
310 N. 2nd Street
Minneapolis, MN 55401

Learning Development Aids (LDA)
Distributed by
Lakeshore Curriculum Materials Center
3695 E. Dominguez Street
Post Office Box 6291
Carson, CA 90749

Milton Bradley, Inc.
Springfield, MA 01101

Modern Education Corporation
Post Office Box 721
Tulsa, OK 74101

Peabody Language Development Kits
American Guidance Service, Inc.
Publishers Building
Circle Pines, MN 55014

Teaching Resources Corp.
100 Boyleston Street
Boston, MA 02116

Trend Enterprises, Inc.
Post Office Box 43073
St. Paul, MN 55165

APPENDIX C
Books for Teachers, Specialists, and Parents

TEACHERS AND SPECIALISTS

Creative Dramatics for the Classroom Teacher by Ruth Heinig and Lyda Stillwell (Englewood Cliffs, NJ: Prentice-Hall, Inc., 1974).

Handbook for Storytellers by Caroline F. Bauer (Chicago: American Library Association, 1977).

Language Handbook: Concepts, Assessment, Intervention by John R. Muma (Englewood Cliffs, NJ: Prentice–Hall, Inc., 1978).

Language Remediation and Expansion: 100 Skill–Building Reference Lists by Catharine S. Bush (Tucson, AZ: Communication Skill Builders, Inc., 1979).

Making Sense: reading comprehension improved through categorization by Christian Gerhard (Newark, Delaware: International Reading Association, 1975).

Stories to Dramatize by Winifred Ward (Anchorage, KY: The Children's Theatre Press, 1952).

Yellow Pages of Learning Resources (Cambridge: Mass.: The MIT Press, 1972).

PARENTS

I Saw a Purple Cow and 100 Other Recipes for Learning by Cole, Haas, Bushnell, Weinberger (Boston, Mass.: Little, Brown and Company, 1972).

Learning Through Play by Jean Marzollo and Janice Lloyd (New York: Harper and Row, 1972).

Parents, Help Your Child to Read: Ideas to use at home by Ellen DeFranco and Evelyn Pickarts (New York: Van Nostrand Reinhold Company, 1972).

Tell Me Why: Answers to Hundreds of Questions Children Ask by Arkady Leckum (New York: Grosset and Dunlap, 1965).

Other products from Communication Skill Builders . . .

LANGUAGE REMEDIATION AND EXPANSION   *by Catharine S. Bush (1979)*

100 skill-building reference lists. Designed to provide resource material for speech-language pathologists, specialists and classroom teachers involved in language remediation and/or expansion. Included are lists of examples and exercises for major skill areas. Suggested activities that precede each list emphasize communicative interaction and experience-based language. Because most of the skills lists are sequenced in order of difficulty, the teacher may begin at the appropriate level for the individual student or group. 216 pages, 8½" x 11", softbound.   **No. 3052 $15**

30,000 SELECTED WORDS ORGANIZED BY LETTER, SOUND AND SYLLABLE
by Valeda D. Blockcolsky, Joan M. Frazer and Douglas H. Frazer (1979)

A must for every communications professional and school, hospital, clinic or office practice. This handy book is alphabetized and organized by initial, medial and final sound positions and into consonant clusters/blends. It includes medial and final sounds not easily found in a standard dictionary and is arranged by number of syllables (1 to 5) in each word to aid the student's progression from simple to complex. There are lists for all spellings for each sound, and sounds are indicated by English letters and phonetic spellings. 600 pages, 4-3/8" x 7-1/4".
No. 2056 $10 (softbound)   **No. 3083 $15** (hardbound)

101 LANGUAGE ARTS ACTIVITIES   *by Trudi Aarons and Francine Koelsch (1979)*

Includes 101 different step-by-step directions for making games, gameboards, and learning centers that can be used by reading, as well as nonreading, children. Because each game is geared to reach a specific performance objective, the materials are ideal for developing IEPs. 134 pages, 8½" x 11", softbound.   **No. 3053 $10**

COMMUNICATIVE COMPETENCE: A FUNCTIONAL–PRAGMATIC APPROACH TO LANGUAGE THERAPY   *by Charlann S. Simon (1979)*

A text for the professional working with school-age children who have not developed meaningful word combinations that allow them to communicate in a variety of settings. Sixteen appendices offer practical information and reproducible administrative forms and more than 150 bibliographical references. Ideal as a text for a college-level course. 128 pages, 8½" x 11", softbound.   **No. 3103 $12.50**

PLANNING INDIVIDUALIZED SPEECH AND LANGUAGE INTERVENTION PROGRAMS   *by Nickola Wolf Nelson (1979)*

This 240-page book provides the professional with time-saving reproducible administrative forms to assist in the writing of IEPs. It is designed to be used by regular classroom teachers, speech-language pathologists, and college students who are learning to plan programs for communicatively handicapped children. A glossary is provided for those who are unfamiliar with some of the professional terminology used in the behavioral objective sequences and explanatory notes. The objectives are remedial in nature and are designed to assist the professional develop desired communicative abilities in areas where a specific disability has been identified. 240 pages, 8½" x 11", wirebound.   **No. 3099 $15**

UN"FAMILIAR" FABLES FOR /s/ CARRYOVER   *by Dianne Schoenfeld Barad (1979)*

Humorous /s/ carryover stories and activities for middle and upper grade level students. Each zany story, the origin of which should be familiar to most students, provides the basis for reinforcement of the objective. In addition to five reproducible stories, there are five 12" x 19" gameboards, fifteen sheets of cut-apart word cards, four gamepieces and five spinner arrow/rivet sets. Manual is 16 pages, 8½" x 11", softbound.   **No. 3102 $15**

Communication Skill Builders, Inc. ®

3130 N. Dodge Blvd./P.O. Box 42050
Tucson, Arizona 85733
(602) 327-6021